Wondrous L

A Gay Pastor's Personal Journey To Acceptance!

A study for ALL people

David J Harvey

ISBN: 1-4775-9835-9
ISBN-13: 9781477598351

dedication: This book is dedicated to the memory of my mother Helen Electa Birchard Harvey and my youngest sister Marlene "Joy" Harvey Bursch.

TABLE OF CONTENTS

acknowledgements: I wish to thank all the many people who have contributed to my understanding down through the years and those who have allowed me to convey these truths.

I also want to thank all those who have read and offered valuable insights on this book's content, and helped me to share them.

Thank you to all those individuals who have supported me over these many years.

CAUTION: This book contains explicit discussions about sexual behavior.

If you are easily offended by such matters, you should *not* proceed further.

I will be getting real and keeping it real!

forward: This book is born out of my great desire to educate my "Christian" friends, as well as those secular friends who have stayed away from spirituality because of the homophobia they saw, and those hopping around from church to church trying to find acceptance and reconcilia-tion between their faith and sexuality. My gay friends and acquaintances continually come up against religious bigotry, preju-dice, racism, intolerance, and bias, all in the name of Christianity. Shall I go on?

The "church" has done terrible harm to the gay and lesbian community either intentionally or unintentionally. It is my desire that the information in this book informs and help the public at large. It is also my desire to help my religious friends, whoever they are, who have not taken the time to understand this complex and sen-sitive subject.

Society at large has been inundat-ed with bigotry because of the negative teachings of the church. I hope to provide some understanding for the broader pub-lic—and the gay and lesbian community as to what the Scriptures actually do and do not say about homosexuality, and about *all* of God's children.

I like to use humor in my preaching style, but don't let that confuse you into thinking that this is not a serious subject. For some people, it has been deadly serious, literally.

I have taught these principles many times throughout the years to the church I pastor, as well as at seminars, conventions, and conferences. This information is based on the work of many scholars and my own personal experience as pastor ministering to the LGBT (Lesbian, Gay, Bi-Sexual and Transgendered) community. I want this book to be read by "ordinary people." I recommend that anyone who is interested in furthering their knowledge on the subject of homosexuality and the Bible refer to the extensive listings at the end of this book, from which I have collected my information.

Also, I am not the final authority or expert on the topic of Christianity and Homosexuality. My life has not always been without involvement, partaking, criticism and blame; however I have always wanted to bring wholeness and healing to my brothers and sisters.

introduction: Let me start by saying that I am a born-again Christian. For those who do not understand that term, it means that I have accepted Jesus Christ as my personal Lord and Savior. I am filled with the Holy Spirit and walk with an awareness of God's presence in my life. I am dedicated to making God's love known and to making His name glorious to all people.

Currently I pastor a gay and lesbian church in San Jose, California. I am humbled by scripture which says that pastors are a gift from the Lord to the church for its edification (teaching). Paul says in *Ephesians* 4:11-13 NIV:

> "So Christ Himself gave the apostles, the prophets, the evangelists, the pastors and teachers to equip His people for works of service, so that the body of Christ may be built up until *we all* reach *unity in the faith* and in the knowledge of the Son of God and become mature, attaining to the whole measure of the fullness of Christ."

I teach people these truths, but the listeners have a responsibility to study the information on their own as well. *2 Timothy 2:15* NIV says:

> "Do your best to present yourself to God as one approved, a workman who does not need to be ashamed and who correctly handles the word of truth."

This book would not have been needed if it were not for our "Christian" friends and ministers who are constantly putting themselves in the position of speaking for God, as if they had a complete understanding of God's heart.

If those who are so convinced that homosexuality is wrong, and that homosexuals should be treated as second class citizens, would instead come alongside the homosexuals in their churches instead of throwing them out, the harm done to those human beings would be minimized.

Many evangelists, priests, pastors and ministers are using their pulpits to reject the LGBT person as a viable part of the body of Christ. So let me ask you. If you are so convinced that homosexuality is wrong, which it is not, *Galatians* 6:1 would nevertheless urge you to restore such people gently and not exclude them.

"Dear brothers and sisters, if another believer is overcome by some sin, you who are godly should gently and humbly help that person back onto the right path. And be careful not to fall into the same temptation yourself." (*Galatians 6:1 NLT*)

The admonition is clear: restore, don't reject! Have these pastors, ministers, and priests not read Psalm 133:1 (Message Bible) that tells us, "How wonderful, how beautiful, when brothers and sisters, friends and neighbors get along?"

This book will hopefully provide information and guidance to everyone. We will see that the Bible does not include homosexuality among the list of sins.

The good news is that evangelicals, who are among my very own friends and colleagues, are beginning to realize that they have failed in so many ways to meet the challenges of the gay and lesbian community. Some of the Protestant and Catholic Christian churches often speak about homosexuality in ways that are vulgar and simplistic, to say the least. I believe some of my "Christian friends" have failed to take into account how their ideas and opinions of sexuality have not changed over the years. They are behind the times in their education and thinking. My understanding my faith and sexuality has indeed changed! I know personally that God loves me for who and what I am! My hope is that the Religious Right will take on this delicate issue in a new and accepting way. I can see that it is not my so-called worldly friends who are having a problem, and neither is it the new generation coming up, as much as it is the "traditional" believers of the church.

Fundamentalist conservative Christians do not acknowledge that we, as God's gay and lesbian believers, can have a relationship with God. We walk in the same grace, with the desire to love and serve God. We know that God loves us and accepts us unconditionally. Many people say they believe something, but they do not know why they believe it or if it is even true. Yet those same people will fight you to the death to make sure their "tradition" is not tampered with.

Some mainline churches often ask, "How could there possibly be gay Christians?" They ask this because the traditional fundamentalist view condemns homosexuality as sinful. Because of this, homosexuality was outlawed for centuries and still is in some places.

Frequently, the media sensationalizes gay people who live on the edge. Society rarely presents positive and wholesome representations of the gay community, and there are hundreds. This is often because of a fear of having homosexuality presented as part of church life and home life—as a normal aspect of society. In case you didn't know, you have actually been living with gay people in your society since the beginning of time. They are often unrecognizable because they are so much like everyone else.

So how do we live out the message of Jesus in today's ever-changing culture? How do we welcome "imperfect people" (which is all of us) to become part of God's church, not only in a spiritual sense, but as active participants engaged in the community? The Bible tells us that "we see through a glass darkly" meaning a poor reflection (*1 Corinthians 13:12, KJV)*. This means that we do not always have a complete understanding or see things from God's perspective. There is quite a lot of heterosexual behavior that is wrong, just as there are behaviors amongst some homosexuals that are wrong. The writers of the Bible were absolutely correct to condemn some of the homosexual behaviors when those behaviors were connected with other sinful behaviors (such as idolatry). The specific acts themselves were wrong because they undermined a trust or relationship, and they undermined the place of God in their lives. But the sexual orientation itself was never wrong!

Always remember: the Gospel is the "Good News"!

If the Bible is the Good News—and it is for everyone—how can we be in the midst of this moral evolution? How can there be different possible and plausible interpretations of scripture? Could it be that we have taken certain scriptures out of context by *not* viewing them in the light of tradition and history of the time? Perhaps we need to look at these scriptures again? Maybe we need to step out of our comfort zone and take a look for ourselves? Perhaps we even need to study these passages for ourselves and not take all opinions from the pulpit as absolute fact.

The Gospel is indeed the Good News. But what exactly does that mean? Various denominations of our Christian brothers and sisters around the country and around the world have interpreted the Gospel in different ways. No wonder we have so many denominations today! We can't agree on a lot of things! So how does one determine the correct interpretation?

Could it be that we have been hearing these scriptures from sources that have misinterpreted them all these years, and we have wrongly believed them?

There are many things that are not explained in scripture. Many scholars continue to disagree and have conflicting opinions about the interpretations of scripture. It is not always easy to find answers regarding sexual intimacy and behavior in the context of scripture. It seems to me that people who use the Bible to say that homosexuality is a sin against God know little or nothing about the passages they are speaking about and their true biblical meaning. So how do we know that they are giving correct information on healing? How do we know that they are giving correct information on salvation? Is everything else preached by those ministers and priests correct?

My opinion is that if you have not walked in my shoes as a gay man, then you do not know all that I have experienced mentally, spiritually, emotionally, and physically. Society has failed to take into account how deeply rooted sexuality is in our identity. That is why I have taken on this immensely sensitive subject of homosexuality and the Bible. I also have written this book for my own selfish reasons. I get tired of gay people always asking if they are going to miss out on Heaven. If there is no male or female identity in heaven *(Galatians 3:28)*, then why would God be concerned when it is about love between two souls on earth now?

This topic has also interested me because I knew personally that God loved me. I knew that God had a plan and purpose for me even though I was a gay man. I needed to know from the Bible how God felt about me and my sexual orientation. Surprisingly enough, I did not find the condemnation that I was hearing from the pulpits and television evangelists, but instead I found acceptance and affirmation. Are you ready for enlightenment?

Chapter 1
Embracing What God Has Made

⊙⊙

Being a homosexual is more than just a sexual behavior. A homosexual is who you are. It is not what you do behind closed doors or with whom you have sex. It is your whole psyche, your entire make-up as a person. It is who you were created to be by God. This is true whether or not you ever act on your homosexuality or whether you are a "practicing" homosexual. You still have a homosexual orientation.

I know that God can use anyone and often does, but there are some people who are ministering in our pulpits today who have caused immeasurable harm. Let me share with you just some of the harm that "Bible-based" homophobia has done by the exclusionary theology that it has preached.

Many times, people believe an anti-gay message simply because it comes from a clergy's teaching. I encourage those in the gay community not to take that false information and apply it to their understanding of Gods acceptance of their sexuality. We have a responsibility to evaluate the message that we hear, regardless of who is delivering it to us.

I know that many of these same "ordained" people, claiming to speak on behalf of God, do not have a sound education on this topic and do not want or even care to understand matters pertaining to the topic of homosexuality. History has proven this over and over again by the countless errors and misunderstanding of doctrine on this and other subjects. Preachers, denominations, and hierarchies have misinterpreted scripture according to their own biases and levels of knowledge. Neither the "Church" nor individual Christians are infallible in what they may say to you or teach as gospel.

People may be shocked by my saying that many Christian preachers are misinformed and behind the times. But this situation has precedent in Christian history. Christians believed for hundreds of years that the Church of Rome was the only valid church. Then the Holy Spirit moved on Martin Luther and taught people that they could reach God directly and not go through a priest. It took a man of courage to stand up and act on what he believed. The Spirit is now moving upon us and showing us a more inclusive way of living out the Christian message.

The book you are about to read is in many ways a restating of years of research done by numerous scholars, theologians and individuals on the subject of homosexuality and the Bible. For me it is the restating of this knowledge from my unique perspective as a preacher of the gospel—a representative of Jesus Christ and a gay man. I hope that I will encourage people to take a different view on this sensitive and confrontational subject.

This book is also based on the various presentations, seminars, and conferences that I have attended, books that I have read, and sermons that I have presented. Many Christian gay people continue to ask the same questions: "Does God love the gay person?" My opinion is that the majority of these people addressing this issue have not taken the time to research the topic. Their opinions are shaped by false information and their own personal biases on this topic. They are too busy to read scripture for themselves. They are going by what "others" have said.

As hard as it is to believe in this modern age, some people in various "Christian" communities have not been exposed to openly gay people. Ironically, they may be personally acquainted with homosexual people but not know it because those homosexuals are hiding their sexuality. Also, some Christians go out of their way to avoid gay people because they see homosexuality as sinful. Some Christians even believe that there is Biblical justification for doing so, which shows that they have not had any sort of correct teaching on the subject. They still use homosexuality as a dividing issue amongst themselves and others. Tragically, many times this occurs even within their personal families. So who is going to be salt and light to these individuals?

There are always going to be people in every community—straight, gay, black, white, Hispanic, Asian, etc.—who are marginalized by others because they belong to minorities. Fortunately, the majority of people within any group or culture are well-meaning individuals who try to live their lives appropriately. But there will always be a few eccentrics in society who will lump together entire groups and cultures, such as homosexuals, into negative stereotypes saying that there is something wrong with all of them. What people miss is the obvious: that God intended human beings to be very diverse. God created diversity! Just look around you!

Again, if you are a straight or LGBT person reading this book, you very well might be at a crossroads in your life right now. Understand that God has a good plan for you. God wants you to be the best you can be, whether you are gay or straight. Having incorrect and condemning tapes running in the back of your mind hinders your ability to be all that you can be and enjoying the good things that God has in store for you. We are all God's children. The LGBT worshippers also fit into the tapestry known as Christianity. Any other point of view simply does not agree with the message of Jesus Christ. In fact, the God of the Universe and of all creation chose you. Read *Psalms* 139. It doesn't matter to God what your appearance is or what color your skin is, or what your strengths and weaknesses are, or even your sexual orientation. The Bible says that God knew you before you were even formed in your mother's womb and approved you. God sent you to earth for a reason. And if God be for you, then who can be against you? You have a purpose, and you have a job to do, particularly in this century. This is a special mission that only you can accomplish. There are people that you will come across in your lifetime that will be affected mostly by you. Isn't that great news? You will touch someone's life in a way that no one else can. You can be somebody's somebody! You may not know it now, but there are people who will come into your life that need what you have to give, no matter what your race, gender, or sexual orientation.

I have watched Reverend Joyce Myers and other ministers for years on TBN. She says that you and I have a destiny. I believe that is true! Keep that in mind as we continue to learn what God has to say about the homosexual.

Hopefully the information in this book will help you by providing gay-friendly explanations of those Bible passages that have been used in the past as justifications to condemn

LGBT folks. You will probably recognize examples from your own life how the homophobic Bible interpretations have hurt you. I hope that you will also see how the gay-friendly explanations help you.

I also want this information to provide you with some moral guidance about practical issues facing every LGBT and straight person. I am trusting that this information will offer you hope, and a way to escape from the guilt and shame that some ministers and society have put on you. I will be focusing on easing LGBT spiritual suffering and educating those who do not know the wondrous love and loving truth. That way you can know God's plan for you!

Words are very powerful. People have said things about me, either to my face or behind my back, that have held me back for years. Like many of you reading this book, my self-esteem and self-confidence became depleted because I did not know how to stop allowing those negative words to keep me from succeeding! As a young child, I felt shame because of the messages I heard from my parents, pastor and Sunday School teachers.

I felt alone and that something was wrong with me. I didn't have the knowledge to explain it to myself. Think how you would feel as a young adolescent to discover you were dealing with homosexual feelings and didn't realize it. It was difficult and sometimes intensely embarrassing. For gay people, those feelings are magnified two or three times when there is also shame involved because of same-sex attraction.

Think about when you were an adolescent. What was the message that the leadership in your church was saying about you or even *to* you? What behavior and expectations did they have for you as an individual? What would it mean to you if you were to hear a negative message from the preacher at your Summer Bible Camp while you were struggling with attractions to people of the same gender? You would feel that you could not date a person you loved. You could never fall in love, and never kiss or hold hands with another person that you were attracted to! (Back in those days we were told that "holding hands leads to having babies.")

When I was in high school there was a boy in my church for whom I had strong feelings! I dreamed about spending the rest of my life with him. Of course I felt that I couldn't act upon those feelings or even share them with him, and for sure I would never have been able to marry the boy that I loved in those days. I was extremely isolated, and as much as it impacted my adolescent years, it has continued to impact my adult years and self-image.

It has taken many years for me to realize how I was indoctrinated by wrong religious teachings about homosexuality. For example, at summer Bible and Youth Camp, anti-gay messages were preached to all the attendees. Those of us who heard those words, both straight and gay, were indoctrinated into a view that excluded anyone who did not fit the accepted norm. This view can lead to bullying and violence amongst young people, which it did in my case. We see signs of depression and potential for suicide in many youth today because of these influences. I experienced all of this and more at this young age. Although these feelings and emotions made me feel ashamed, I also knew in my heart that God had His hand on me and loved me. I didn't know how to deal with the conflicts, and I had no one with whom

I could discuss my feelings. I thought it was just a cross I had to bear.

Today there are gay-straight associations in schools to provide a safe place. There are also gay leaders speaking out about their journeys and telling the youth, "Things will get better." There are a growing number of groups, such as the recent Trevor project, that have been providing information and support to youth across the country.

Religious and non-religious homophobias have even turned the neutral word "gay" into an insult. Many young people are taunted by being called "gay," and they feel a need to deny it. Even many youth who *are* gay cannot admit it! This promotes fear and depression. Wouldn't it be so much better if being called "gay" wasn't considered a slur?

My biggest anxiety as a youth was that I would be rejected by my peers, and even by my family. My solution was to conform to the standards I had been taught, even though my solution meant living a lie. I was called a maverick, or nonconformist, a lot of the time. I guess you can tell how that went for me. No wonder there are numerous closeted LGBT people who are prone to lie and tell untruths. It can turn into a survival technique that is carried into adulthood. I was deceiving myself and others around me. Every time I entered a room, the conversation stopped. I was fearful that everyone knew my secret and was thinking, "He's gay!" "We're not sure about him!"

These messages led to low self-esteem and even self-loathing. This inhibited my success in every aspect of my life. It had a ripple effect in all that I did. I didn't start feeling good about myself until I was in junior high when I discovered I had musical and artistic talent. But, by then, it was too late to erase the negative tapes that were already playing in my conscious and subconscious mind. Those negative tapes still pop up occasionally today, but now, with the knowledge I have acquired on homosexuality and the Bible, I am able to live a productive life. Hopefully this book will help some of you, my readers, overcome these same issues for yourselves. I want you to take heart in the many recent stories about gay leaders, actors, musicians, and others who have struggled for years in silence who are now coming forward to share their stories—many times at great cost personally and professionally.

Arrogant, self-righteous, and judgmental Christianity is simply unchristian.

I hope that you can begin to see God as a good God, a God who heals you from your past, and a God who will walk with you and be there as your friend now and in the future. *Other people's rejection of you will not change God's love for you.* Let the hurt go, and receive the love and healing that God has for you each and every day.

Chapter 2
Starting The Journey

I was born on an army base in Richland, Washington where my father was serving in the Army. Shortly afterwards we moved to Buffalo, Montana, population 30, to take over my grandparents' farm. At age five I started school in a one-room county school house that still exists today. The elementary grades were all combined in one room.

One day, our family visited another family's home in the area. They had a son who was in an upper grade. I knew him from school and liked him. He took me out to a bunk house to play, and there I lost my innocence. His game was to actually rape me. All I could remember was the pain. At this point in my life, I had no one to tell. The next day we played at the school yard as if nothing had happened. He hugged me and held me as we came down the fire escape together. I loved that.

Recent studies indicate that being sexually assaulted as a child may cause over-sexualizing throughout the victim's life. It's like your soul has been imprinted and magnetized for inappropriate sexual expression, whether heterosexual or homosexual. There may not even be an understanding of what draws you to such behavior. It just is.

Less than two years later when I was seven, my mother moved me and my sister to Lewistown, Montana. There we rented a house from my Grandma Moran. My brother had a much closer relationship with my father, so he stayed with him on the farm. By then, my parent's relationship was already being challenged. My dad wanted to stay on the farm but my mother did not. The farm was losing money so they decided to sell. My mother moved my sister and me into Lewistown, until other arrangements could be made. Eventually they sold the farm. But it was in Lewistown that I then began to deal socially with the issue of being gay when I was only in the first grade.

I was on the playground with a young friend of mine. He told me that his mother said he could not play with me anymore because I was a "homosexual." (Don't you just love the small town gossip?) This family knew nothing about me, yet there was already something about me that let people know I was different. Even back then I must have had a neon sign on my head that said "Queer!" So I asked my mother, "What's a homosexual?" She passed it off and said that kids are just mean. It was my first inkling that homosexuality was considered a bad thing.

During all of this time, I was growing up in a Christian home. My mother made sure that I went to Sunday school and learned the basic truths of the Bible. From an early age I understood the concept of sin, right and wrong and eternal punishment. I wanted to be a good boy. At a community wide prayer meeting that my mother attended regularly, I invited Jesus into my heart and was filled with the Holy Spirit. Despite all this, as I grew older, sexual questions kept coming up in my mind, and the memory of the pain of the rape confused me. There was no one to help me understand that event.

Some people might assume that I became a homosexual because I was raped. It is more basic than that. At the age of five, to the best of my memory, I had no conscious attraction to anyone, although I did like playing with dolls and I got dressed up! I also like playing doctor. I liked how some other boys looked and wanted to be accepted by them, but it was only later that I began to feel actual physical attraction towards members of the same sex. The rape was painful, but the attraction which arose in later years was pleasant. So today I still don't see a connection between the rape and my sexual orientation.

Throughout my junior and senior high school years, I had sexual experiences with boys and girls in the neighborhood. In my day we called that playing doctor. It only confirmed to me that I was "different" and attracted to same-sex encounters. I never felt like there was anyone to tell about my puzzlement of attraction. On one occasion, as a way to try to be like the other boys, I had a sexual experience with a girl in the neighborhood. I only felt guilty afterwards and inwardly vowed not to do that again. I didn't have that same guilt with my male experiences which felt very natural to me. Many boys have these kinds of experiences as they go through puberty.

I graduated from high school in 1974. Because of my family connection to the Assembly of God ("A/G") church, it was a natural step for me to attend the A/G's bible college in Kirkland, Washington—Northwest Bible College. I was overjoyed at the thought of leaving the limits of Lewistown. I was hopeful that all of the emotional conflicts of my youth would be left behind as well.

One day in my sophomore year at Northwest, I was called unexpectedly into the Dean's office. I couldn't understand why I was being summoned. I was an upstanding scholarship student, and my school bill was paid, thanks to my parents pre-planning. I was vice president of my sophomore class and was on the student council, as well as representing the college in a traveling musical group. I couldn't figure out why I was being called in. I was nervous when I entered the Dean's office.

The dean got right to the point. No "Hi-how-are-you?" "How is college life treating you?" He told me that my traveling bed partner had reported that he and I had had a sexual experience together. My bed partner was feeling guilty about it.

To give you some background, as traveling musicians representing the A/G College, we music students were often housed in host homes. We would typically sleep two to a bed. Of course, the boys would sleep with the boys and the girls with the girls. The problem was that we were all sexually mature 18 or 19-year old youths with raging hormones.

On the night in question, the boy in bed with me had become sexually aroused. He started rubbing his erected penis against my buttocks, which woke me up. I turned over to him to help him with the process, but he would become inhibited when he was just about ready to ejaculate. So I turned back over and tried to go back to sleep, but he started rubbing against me again. I decided to accommodate him again by masturbating him. Once I had relieved him, we were both able to fall asleep. He became cold and distant to me after this all happened. He approached me later when we were back at school and said "Let's go tell the Dean what we've done." I said no! Let's just forget it ever happened! He said he couldn't.

You may wonder how college personnel could be so naïve about puberty. It is natural for boys our age to get horny with another body in bed with us. Well, the college administrators really *were* that naïve because sexuality was not a topic of discussion in our classes, churches or in our homes. All sexuality outside of the marriage covenant was considered sinful. End of discussion! It was difficult to talk about this subject because we thought that it would lead to sins of lust and desire. We were on our honor as good Christian men and women representing the college to always be Christian in our behavior. That meant no sex unless we were married. Of course sex was going on with the other Christian college students all the time.

The message the Dean gave me was this: "We don't accept *gay* people at this college." He pressed me further, "Do you know anyone else on this campus that is gay? I was living off campus at the time. The administration had already heard that this type of behavior was going on in the dorms. (Dorms I thought! It's going on in the back parking lots and in the woods above the chapel.) It is unacceptable for you to be representing the college and be engaged in *homosexual* behavior! We want to deal with this problem right now."

He paused. "Homosexual behavior while representing this college is not healthy for you or the reputation of this school." His face was red with anger.

I wasn't the only gay student at the college or representing the college, and I knew who the others were. We all strove to live chaste lives as good Christians, but I wouldn't betray or expose any of my fellow students. I was heartbroken. I believed that my life was over and that I was a complete sinner. It could not be right with God if I were practicing homosexuality.

But as the old saying goes, when God closes a door He opens a window. That is exactly what happened for me! I happened to receive a letter from Evangel College inviting me to attend. Evangel College is located in Springfield, Missouri. This is the same city the headquarters for the Assemblies Of God are located. Even in the midst of my situation, God was lovingly looking out for my welfare. But that still meant more trials and troubles for me.

Sexuality, especially homosexuality, was *not* part of the curriculum at Evangel College either. I carried the same fear of exposure and shameful condemnation the whole time I was there. I did not stop looking however. Sometimes I felt like I had a neon sign around my neck saying, "I am a closeted homo fag." That's how badly I thought of myself.

After three years at Evangel College, I graduated with a B.A. in Music and Education. My next position after college was in Fredonia, Kansas, followed by several other ministerial positions. I experienced the same sorts of problems in every Christian venue that I entered. Other Christians would sense that I was different and that I was more than likely struggling with my sexual identity. This occurred not only as a youth but into my adult years. "Christian" men who were supposedly heterosexual would take advantage of that knowledge and invite me to engage in sexual activities. Most of the time I was offended. I turned down the advances because I was trying to be a "good" Christian. But at the same time, I knew I would have welcomed any sort of intimacy.

There is much more of this activity going on in the Christian community than people are willing to recognize. Why? In my opinion, it is because "traditional" Christians have not been taught or been given the opportunity to discuss these topics in a *safe* environment. They experiment on their own in a hidden manner.

In the early 1970's, it was recognized by psychiatrists and psychologists that homosexuality is *not* a form of mental illness, and it was removed from their diagnostic manual. Praise the Lord! Psychologists have recognized that puberty brings with it a natural interest in sex and a desire to start experimenting. This is just how God created us.

There is a reason for the pleasurable sensations that come with puberty. The human race would not continue if humans did not find sex pleasurable! This is one of the reasons why in Biblical days, people were married at an earlier age, and why bar-mitzvah and bat-mitzvah are done at age 13 for boys and 12 for girls. I'm not saying that we should change the age of consent or the age of marriage. I am not speaking against the wisdom of straight people getting married before having sex since it so often brings a new life into this world. I am just saying that we should be realistic and knowledgeable about what is happening in the human body as we go through puberty.

As an adult, I continued to assume leadership roles in churches. I usually served in a dual role as a music minister and education director at Sunday school, vacation Bible school, summer camps, Royal Rangers and Missionettes. Looking back on this I find it ironic that I was leading and teaching people when I was so confused myself!

In the Assembly of God church, when a senior pastor leaves, all of his staff is expected to resign as well. That leaves a new pastor with the freedom to choose his own staff. I experienced this in 1986 when I unexpectedly had to leave my position as music minister in Antioch, California, because the pastor decided to retire. (Antioch, by the way, was named after the city where the followers of Jesus were first called Christians.) I went to live with my mother who by that time had moved to San Jose, California.

Because of this constant upheaval in my life, I decided to more closely examine the subject of homosexuality and how it applied to me as a Christian gay man. I knew I loved God and God loved me. I was filled with the Holy Spirit, but I was not able to put together what people were saying about my effeminate traits and how God created me. I went through a time of severe depression. I felt isolated from my faith and my Christian church family even while I was still attending a local church.

Around that same time, I was asked to house-sit for an elderly couple who were taking a vacation for several months. Alone in their home, I fasted and prayed. It gave me some inkling of how Jesus must have felt when He was in the desert for forty days as He fasted and prayed about His future. But I also began to search for other gay people with whom to develop friendships and relationships. I was still in the closet about my homosexual orientation and wanted some form of anonymity.

During this search, I discovered the personal ads in the local newspaper and magazines: men seeking women, men seeking men, etc. In those days before the internet, you either wrote a few letters back and forth before meeting, or you would make that first initial telephone call. Much to my surprise, there were a few ads that had "spiritual" comments in their content. When I contacted those people and explained my circumstances, several relationships blossomed! One of those people was an Episcopalian minister who would change my life.

Chapter 3
God Delivers The Answers

My new Episcopalian friend that I met through the personal ads, was a minister who served his church in various capacities. He conducted Bible study classes at his home where a few men would show up to discuss the Bible and have fellowship. He was a wonderful teacher with an extraordinary knowledge of the Word, but I still questioned his Biblical explanations on the topic of homosexuality. As you know, I grew up in the Assemblies of God, and we were always leery of people—even other Christians—who were not of our same denomination or belief system. I was afraid that his liberal Episcopalian interpretations might be delusions from the devil! After one of those meetings I asked him to show me how he personally came to terms with his homosexuality and being a Christian, and a minister no less!

In the Assemblies of God, we take people through four steps to salvation. These four steps are found in John's Gospel, and they lead to an understanding of Jesus Christ:

- God loves you and has a wonderful plan for your life.
- Man is corrupt and separated from God. You can't experience God's love for your life without faith in Jesus Christ.

- Jesus Christ is God's only provision for man's offense—the only way to Heaven.
- We must individually receive Jesus Christ as Savior and Lord.

I remembered these steps from my teachings in evan-
gelism class at Northwest Bible College. In fact, we had gone
on the streets and presented this information in downtown
Seattle on several occasions. So I had already gotten the
idea that there must be some step-by-step process for understanding how a person who is homosexual finds acceptance in Christ.

Sure enough, my new Episcopalian friend had a process that worked for him. He walked me through a biblical
foundation of God's love for every person. After hearing that
information, I felt a big burden lift from me. This was a real
revelation! I was so thrilled that I could be gay and Christian
at the same time. I was finally going to be free of my struggle
and live in the *truth* of God's love! I was very impressed by
the fact that he based all that he said on a close study of the
scriptures and was not "off" in his views. He began by taking
me to *Genesis* chapter 2.

He said, and I hope I remember it correctly, that the
story of Adam and Eve emphasized that their attraction to
each other was based on sameness. (*Genesis* 2:19-20). God
declared that it was not good for Adam to be alone. The animals were certainly not enough to fulfill all of his physical,
psychological, and social needs. After all, Adam was made in
the image of God, not the animals. He needed someone like
himself, taken out of his own side—the "bone of my bone
and flesh of my flesh."

With Adam and Eve, God created marriage as the first institution between humans. As my friend explained to me, this does not only mean male-female relationships, but it also refers to male-male relationships since later in Scripture, Laban calls *his nephew* "bone of my bone and flesh of my flesh," which uses the same Hebrew words to identify the intimate connection. (*Genesis* 29) The same Hebrew words are used in both stories to identify the intimate connection. Many right- wing preachers like to say, "It's Adam and Eve, not Adam and Steve." They ignore one little thing. God gave those genes to Adam and Eve to give us Adam and Steve; Sally and Susie.

Evangelical fundamentalists frequently use this part of the Bible to support the idea that only men and women should be married. However, the Bible, such as in *Acts 10:15 NIV,* declares that what God has made and said is clean...is clean! If the homosexual is in Christ, then they are accepted as God's very own! What God has called clean we should not call unclean. Equality is for all!

Since eunuchs do not procreate, does that mean that their intimate feelings of love are meant to be suppressed and bear no spiritual fruit? No! God created certain men and women as "eunuchs." Jesus said,

"For there are eunuchs who were born that way, and there are eunuchs who have been made eunuchs by others—and there are those who choose to live like eunuchs (homosexuals) for the sake of the kingdom of heaven. The one who can accept this should accept it." (*Matthew 19:12*)

God has gifted eunuchs with feelings of love. Some are born eunuchs, some achieve eunuch status and some have eunuch status thrust on them; many consider homosexuals today to be what Jesus referred to as eunuchs."

Then he took me to *Leviticus* 18. Here we found a list of sexual taboos, but there are biblical exceptions. *Leviticus 18* forbids the uncovering of the nakedness of a half-sister by a half-brother, yet God promised Abraham and Sara the child Isaac. (From *Halley's Bible Handbook, Genesis 20:12*) They were a half-sister and half-brother couple, yet God did not exclude them or reject them from His promises.

In another example, *Leviticus 18:16* forbids the uncovering of your brother's wife. Yet *Deuteronomy 25* allows a man to marry his brother's wife upon the death of his brother if they had not had any children. This way the widow would have some children to carry on the blood line and care for her in old age. In the social pecking order of the day, women were considered property, beneath the value of livestock, and this was one way for widows to have protection and a roof over their heads. This was in the context of the culture of the time.

This was all information that I had never thought about before. I had already studied these passages in Sunday School and college, and I knew this was what the Bible said. But I had never heard them interpreted that way. I felt in my heart that my friend was correct!

My friend also pointed out that the Bible was full of sex and violence. I had never looked at the Bible in that light before either. One example my friend showed me was the story of Tamar and Amnon. Tamar was King David's daughter, and her half-brother Amnon was in love with her. To avoid the stigma of being raped by Amnon, Tamar knew her father would not stop her from marrying Amnon. Amnon, however, refused to listen to Tamar and raped her anyway. His lust changed to disgust almost immediately and he threw her from the room. She was forced to live in disgrace. (*2 Samuel 13*) David's son Absalom gave her shelter, and for two years. Absalom's hatred for Amnon boiled inside his heart. Family drama just like what is experienced today. One day Absalom went out with his sheep shearers and took Amnon with him. Absalom instructed his men to wait until Amnon was drunk with wine and then to strike him down. They did as they were commanded. It could be a story of sex and violence from our own daily newspaper.

I began to realize that just as there are exceptions to almost all civil and criminal laws today, there were exceptions to God's laws in the Old Testament! God understood that people's circumstances would be different, given the culture and the context of His laws. The world has always been changing.

Then my friend showed me positive examples of relationships in the Bible that were more than likely homosexual! The relationship between David and Jonathan was one of those examples. I will go into more detail later in the book. I always suspected there was more to their friendship than what I was being told!

In my mind, I began to think the unthinkable: Could it really be that God loves the homosexual as much as He loves the heterosexual? Does He really have a plan and purpose for my life?

I was reminded of *Jeremiah 29:11:*

"For I know the plans that I have for you, sayeth the Lord, they are plans for good and not for evil to give you a future and to give you a hope."

Could it really be that Gods plan was to use the homosexual in His Kingdom here on earth? Why would God allow these examples to remain in the Bible if He condemns homosexuality? I was starting to find out the truth!

My friend and I examined Paul's letter to the church at Rome. The first chapter of *Romans* is often used as a "clobber passage" to condemn homosexual behavior, but I started to see something different there. I'll share more details with you in upcoming chapters.

This was all too much. It was new information that I had never heard before, or interpreted this way, but in my spirit, I felt and knew it to be true. My mind was just overwhelmed! How is it that this information was never shared in this light by any of the churches or colleges that I had attended? Were they trying to hide something or use the Law to keep people under bondage? I realized that God *does* love me just the way He created me! I experienced more freedom in my relationship with God than I'd ever known before. I could now live as a gay Christian man with no guilt or shame. I was going to make my mess my message!

After I learned these things from my mentor, I realized that there was a need for another Bible-based study group to reach even more people with this information on these issues, so I began one in my own home. Word of my group began to spread as I visited at gay-affirming churches and told them what I was trying to accomplish. I attended a gay Christian conference in San Jose, and after that to a gay church and then a national gay Christian conference in Texas.

It finally came to me that my mission was to do more than just a Bible study, but to start a full Bible-based gay congregation in San Jose. This was confirmed to me through conversations at the Texas conference from many other people who told me that my personal gifts and insights, leadership and talents, would be useful in ministry. They encouraged me to step out in ministry as a pastor. They had no idea that I was already considering such a thing. I gathered some supportive people around me and began the process.

This process of awakening and self-acceptance caused me to realize that many homosexuals have been unfairly harmed and driven away from God. The reason I believe that I remained faithful to the church was because of my mother's influence. I met people who had stopped being religious, and even stopped seeking a relationship with God, because scriptures were used negatively against them.

A pastor at one of the churches I attended in San Jose would always say, "There is a God-shaped hole in the heart of every person that only God can fill!" Although we have different faith journeys, we all desire a relationship with God, and we long to develop spiritually. It saddened my heart that so many LGBT people were being driven out of churches and not offered the same opportunity to have an intimate relationship with the Lord Jesus Christ. People in the gay and lesbian community often need help finding churches that are open and affirming, and that celebrate them as part of the faith community. We long for a faith family that will not just tolerate us but that will actually celebrate who we are as gay Christians. Tolerance is just a watered down word for grace. Either you want grace exclusively or you want grace with a little "law" mixed in with it so you can tell people if there are right or wrong.

To the gay individual reading this book, I would hope you find a church where you are celebrated, and not just tolerated. After all, in a way, heterosexuals are celebrated in the churches because they celebrate the union of men and women. Gay people make their own contributions to our society, so we should all be celebrated, not just tolerated.

To the straight person reading this book, I would ask: who is going to be the salt and light to the gay person in your midst? If you feel that homosexuality is so wrong, why haven't you as a mature Christian become salt and light to these individuals? It seemed even more tragic that LGBT people were allowing an important and deep part of them— their sexual orientation—to become a stumbling block to being a genuinely committed Christian.

Those were the seed ideas that made me decide to create a church upholding those concepts. I felt that God was calling me "for such a time as this" *(Esther 4:14)*—a phrase that has become popular with the Christian community today.

I realized that you can't change your past, but you can do something about the future. I know that throughout your life you have encountered forces and people who opposed you and tried to keep you in the dark places. I write these words to encourage you to start resisting those things, and begin to see yourself as God sees you. It is the job of the enemy to keep you so discouraged and defeated that you won't even attempt to live for God.

Please know that God wants to restore you to fellowship with Himself. God is a restorer! God wants to do a new thing in you. God wants you to have hope for a brighter future. Let these thoughts go deep inside your spirit. Let them grow and blossom.

Scripture says: "No weapon formed against you will prosper." And "It's the goodness of the Lord that draws people to repentance", not people condemning you. (*Romans 2:4, KJV*). It is not the browbeating that you may be receiving from your church family and friends that will cause you to love Him! God said He would turn your situation around. You have and will continue to see positive changes in society and in attitudes towards gay and lesbian people as you allow the love of God to fill your heart and life. Just be patient.

So let's look at the passages in the Bible that made me conclude that people can be gay and Christian at the same time. When others try to use any of those scripture passages as weapons against you, your spirit will know how wrong they are.

Chapter 4
It's The Context, Silly!

It is my desire in writing this book to educate and help you grow mentally, spiritually, and emotionally! It is also to help you know and understand the *context* in which the scriptures were written. From this point on, I will be using the same tools that the "Religious Right" people have used. I will show you what Scripture *really* means in regard to our place as gay and lesbian Christians and straight Christians.

The church where I pastor believes that the Bible is correct, as long as it is translated *correctly*:

> "But you must continue in the things which you have learned and been assured of, knowing from whom you have learned them, and that from childhood you have known the Holy Scriptures, which are able to make you wise for salvation through faith which is in Christ Jesus. All Scripture is given by inspiration of God, and is profitable for doctrine, for reproof, for correction, for instruction in righteousness, that the man of God may be complete, thoroughly equipped for every good work." *(2 Timothy 3:14-17 NIV)*

Here is something that is very important to understand if you are to gain confidence and understanding on this matter of one's sexual orientation and as a child of the living God: The Word of God is infallible, perfect, dependable, and trustworthy when you go back to the original text and understand the context in which it was written. Many theologians who have studied the scriptures for years will emphasize the need to always take scripture in *context*.

Did I happen to mention the word "context"?

When studying the Bible, we should never translate or apply individual Bible verses in isolation. As Dr. Joseph Pearson has stated in his seminars, "One needs to understand the context in which it was written both literally and historically." I have heard it said that "to proof-text without context is pretext."

People have been using scripture to support all sorts of beliefs. Some of those beliefs are correct, others are not. I hope that your faith in Jesus Christ will be strengthened and your knowledge of God's Word will be deepened as you delve into this important subject.

As part of this training, I recommend that you have some good study tools to keep you on track. This is important for every serious Bible student. I recommend these four basic texts, especially when you are studying controversial topics:

A.   A good Bible dictionary, such as *Vine's Complete Expository Dictionary of Old and New Testament*

B.   A concordance such as *Strong's New Exhaustive Concordance.* A concordance can be an invaluable tool to understanding words, phrases and terms in the Bible.

C.   A good commentary of which there are many in most Bible book stores. This is a series of notes explaining or interpreting a written text. I might suggest a *Matthew Henry's* commentary or even the *New International Bible Commentary.* They both are good for study for the casual Bible student.

D.   A multi-translation Bible or "Parallel Bible" is also very helpful.

These books will be very helpful to you in understanding the meaning of any word.

When using these tools, ask yourself these questions:

1.   What does this passage teach in the context in which it was written?

2.   Are there other passages in Scripture that can "back up" the passage you are reading? Two or three passages from scripture give you greater assurance that the Bible really means what you think it does. See *Matthew 18:16* and *Hebrews 10:28.*

3.   How does the passage, written thousands of years ago, apply to you today personally in the 21st century, or does it apply at all?

4.   What does the passage reveal about Jesus Christ?

5.   Is this passage to be taken literally? Someone once said that people have a tendency to speak symbolically but they understand literally.

Most people who make a serious study of the Bible follow these practices. You can think of the same questions in these terms:

1.   Determine *to whom* the passage was originally written.

2.   Determine *who* wrote the passage.

3.   Determine *why* the passage was written.

4. Determine *what* the circumstances were that sur-
    rounded the writing of the passage.

One of the obstacles we face when studying the passages about sexual conduct is that the original text was written in Hebrew (Old Testament) and Greek (New Testament).
Only later, and I mean much later, was the first English version of the Bible assembled in 1534 A.D. (the Coverdale Bible,
ancestor to the King James Version). Right or wrong, many
of our present day doctrines are based on these early translations, or offshoots of these works.

And here is what is amusing: King James, the very person who had the Bible translated for the common people,
was a known homosexual! (*God's Secretaries,* p. 60). Didn't I
say that gays have made big contributions to society, even
to the service of God? Much more is coming up!

Bible interpreters today do not have an easy task. In
many cases, the old English words used in the King James
version and other early translations have little or no meaning
to us today (*e.g.,* the word "catamite"), or the meanings have
totally changed (*e.g.,* "effeminate"), much like the game gossip. In many cases, the original text was meant to be used in
a figurative rather than in a literal sense.

A good illustration is the schoolroom command, "All
eyes on the chalkboard." In a literal sense, students are being asked to physically place their eyes in contact with the
chalkboard. In the figurative sense, this phrase means, "Look
at the chalkboard and give me your undivided attention."

Our biggest challenge lies in the fact that the English
language is often limited when compared to the Greek. A
good example is the word "love." In the Greek language,

there are at least three different words to describe various forms of love that are translated into the single word "love" in English versions of scripture. This is not very descriptive and cannot begin to convey the levels of intensity with which we may love someone or something. These are the major Greek words for love in the New Testament:

- *Philia*—Friendship—love between family and friends.
- *Eros*—Romance—love in the sense of 'Being in love.' An emotional connection with another person.
- *Agape*—Unconditional Love—love regardless of circumstance.

You can see why during translation, verses can be inadvertently given meanings that were never intended in the original. In other words, God's perfect word may get muddied when man attempts to give the Lord a helping hand in translating His book! This is very obvious with the scriptures that many people associate with homosexuality.

Finally, we need to use a *common sense* approach to interpreting the Bible. God isn't going to tell us something "out in left field." Every interpretation must line up with other scriptural truths and commandments, such as the laws of love. God is not the author of confusion *(1 Corinthians 14:33)* and "every matter must be established by the testimony of two or three witnesses." (2 *Corinthians 13:1)*. In short, scripture will interpret scripture, and our conclusions should make logical sense. If they don't, then we have missed the target and need to start again. So, let's start!

Chapter 5
"Getting It" In Sodom!

Most of us know the story of Sodom and Gomorrah. For the gay and lesbian person reading this book, and for those who love them, this is probably one of the most important topics you will study in all your life. If you truly understand the story of Sodom, it will change you, your friends, and your community. This is going to be a long discussion, so put your brains in motion.

The gay Christian community has been attacked by the mainstream "Christian" church over this one story for years. Because of this misinterpretation of scripture, many LGBT persons have been rejected by their own families, friends, and church. Gay people who might otherwise be drawn to Jesus Christ exclude themselves from Christian fellowship because *they think* they are supposed to be something different than what and who they actually are.

Before going further, let's make one fact perfectly clear: the Bible is *not* a textbook on sex. It is not the *Kama Sutra,* even though there is a lot of sexual content. The Bible is not a sex manual any more than it is a textbook on mathematics or geography. The main purpose of the Bible is to present God's love and plan of salvation for humanity as it has been demonstrated throughout history, and as it applies to the context of our times today.

Within the Pentecostal and Evangelical churches, people have been taught with conviction that the "sin" of homosexuality caused the destruction of Sodom and Gomorrah. My mother told me that the downfall of a nation was because of homosexuality. The story has been used by many preachers as "proof text" to condemn the homosexual. That teaching is a lie straight from the pit of Hell! Why would a preacher of the gospel tell such a lie? "God is not a God that He should lie." (*Numbers 23:19*) Many of those preachers are actually well-meaning people, but they just haven't done their research correctly.

I have attended various workshops, and read history books surrounding this matter. I have also listened to theologians who are skilled in reading and understanding Greek and Hebrew. I have arrived at my conclusions as to what scripture actually says based on these influences on this subject. You should become familiar with such authors as John Boswell, Mel White, Dr. Joseph Pearson, and Samuel Kader, Elaine Sunby—among others. That is one way you can become knowledgeable about these passages and try to understand and share their truths.

Let's look at the *context* of the Sodom story. I am sure homosexuality occurred in that city. Homosexuality has occurred since the beginning of time, but that was not the reason that God destroyed the city.

First of all, current statistics say that one out of every ten people in the world is homosexual, maybe even a few less than that. So, how many homosexuals would there have been in Sodom? When someone falsely tells you that the *entire city* was homosexual, it is said for *shock value. It cannot possibly be true.* So the fundamental problem is misinformation about sexual orientation, and the historical and cultural contexts of this and other Bible stories.

As we review the history at that time, we see several things. In Genesis, we have discovered that Gods judgment on Sodom and Gomorrah was pronounced long before that judgment was actually carried out. You need to remember, know and understand this fact before you can fully understand this story. It is necessary to know the background, the context, the times, and the culture in which it was written.

Sodom was located at the end of the Dead Sea. It was a fertile land. The people of Sodom enjoyed "great prosperity." This suggests that there was a surplus of goods. Because of their great wealth, the people became arrogant, conceited, proud, overconfident and self-seeking. This sounds like some of our major cities today.

Genesis 13:5-9 records the story of Lot and his Uncle Abraham as they came to the Promised Land:

> "Lot also, who went with Abram, had flocks and herds and tents. Now the land was not able to support them that they might dwell together, for their possessions were so great that they could not dwell together. And there was strife between the herdsmen of Abram's livestock and the herdsmen of Lot's livestock. The Canaanites and the Perizzites then dwelt in the land.
> So Abram said to Lot, "Please let there be no strife between you and me, [good advice to 'Christians' today] and between my herdsmen and your herdsmen; for we are brethren. Is not the whole land before you? Please separate from me. If you take the left, then I will go to the right; or, if you go to the right, then I will go to the left." (*Genesis 13:5-9* (NIV)

Abraham and his nephew Lot had had a disagreement, a difference of opinion, a falling out, so they did the sensible thing: they separated peaceably. People today often do that type of thing, but all too often it is not peaceable.

> "Lot looked around and saw that the whole plain of the Jordan toward Zoar was well watered, like the garden of the LORD, like the land of Egypt. (This was before the LORD destroyed Sodom and Gomorrah.) So Lot chose for himself the whole plain of the Jordan and set out toward the east. The two men parted company." *(Genesis 13:10-11 (NIV)*

Notice that Lot and Abram (Abraham) parted as friends. They still had affection for each other. They did the right thing.

Sodom was located on those plains which contained five cities: Sodom, Gomorrah, Adma, Zebulum, and Zoar. Scripture details the lifestyle of the people that lived there: "Now the people of Sodom were wicked and were sinning greatly against the LORD." (*Genesis 13:13 (NIV)*

We know from history and tradition that the people of Sodom worshipped various types of false idols. Historians tell us that the religious practices consisted of numerous rituals, endless sacrifices, and acts of ritual sex. I'll bet that their Sunday morning services were packed!

The Bible tells us that without God, the human heart and mind can become exceedingly depraved, immoral, and wicked:

> "Then the LORD said, The outcry against Sodom and Gomorrah is so great and their sin so grievous that I

will go down and see if what they have done is as bad
as the outcry that has reached me. If not, I will know."
(*Genesis 18:20-21 (NIV)*)

Whenever you see the word "outcry" in scripture, it
means that there had to be victims, people who were wounded: sufferers. There's never an outcry without victims. The
Bible says that the foul odor of Sodom had reached even to
the nostrils of God concerning their depravity. (*Genesis18-19*)

Obviously, something more is going on here in Sodom.
Some have suggested that perhaps sexual abuse was preva-
lent. The culture in Sodom had an accepted practice of rape
and violence as a form of dominance over others. Abuse in
any form is totally different than a loving relationship between two consenting adults.

The Bible tells us that God sent angels disguised as human men to visit Lot in Sodom. According to some translations of the Bible, the people of Sodom saw the angels and
wanted to have sex with them, unaware that they were messengers from God:

"And they called unto Lot, and said unto him, "Where
are the men which came in to thee this night? Bring
them out unto us, that we may know them." (*Genesis
19:5 KJV*)

"Know" is what Joseph did to Mary when he had sexual
intercourse with her after the baby Jesus was born. "Know"
in this context didn't mean, "Let's get acquainted at the local
coffee shop"! The people of Sodom didn't understand that
these men were angels. Their intent was to have forcible

sexual intercourse to assert their supremacy. That meant rape—gang rape.

So their motivation was not homosexual love and emotional attachment, it was domination. As history has demonstrated, what better way is there to humiliate someone than to sexually abuse them against their will? Male or female. This equally applies to heterosexual rape as it does to homosexual rape.

As much as I hate to say this, I do know that homosexual rape occurs. It often takes place in the prisons. Men raping men is very common as a show of dominance, power, and control in the prison environment. The great majority of those men are not homosexual. They are heterosexual.

To prevent this sacrilege, Lot offered his daughters to the mob hoping it would appease them: *WHAT?*

> "Look, I have two daughters who have never slept with a man. Let me bring them out to you, and you can do what you like with them. But don't do anything to these men, for they have come under the protection of my roof." *(Genesis 19:8)*

Why is it that we don't look at Lot with disgust, that he would even consider offering his own children to be abused by sexually violent men? One reason is that women were considered as nothing: they were just property in that day. Can you imagine women today being used like that? I don't think that would go over too well in the women's movement!

This is what I find interesting about the people who present the story as a commentary on the topic of homosexuality: If homosexuality was the only sexual orientation in Sodom, why would Lot have offered his virgin *daughters* to homosexuals who only want to have sex with *men?* To me, that makes no sense at all. If there were only gay men outside the door, which is why some people today think the city was destroyed, then why would Lot offer his daughters? Have you ever stopped to think about that? Did Lot think he could convert a mob of homosexuals into becoming hetero-sexuals that way? Of course not!

In fact, the Bible says in *Genesis 19* that *all* the people of Sodom were there. There were men, women, and chil-dren. It was a mob with a mob mentality, not a bunch of sex-starved, sex-depraved gay men, as some Christians would have us believe. The men in the crowd were mostly hetero-sexual, and they got the idea to gang rape the visitors as a show of domination over an enemy. Instead, the two angels smote them with blindness. Then the angels told Lot to take his family and leave immediately.

There's another important aspect to the sin of Sodom and Gomorrah. Let's look at the passage again when Lot pleads with the mob outside his home:

> "But don't do anything to these men, for they have come under the protection of my roof." (*Genesis 19:8*)

Remember that the heavenly visitors appeared as hu-man beings. Lot recognized that they were from God, and he welcomed them. He invited them to stay for dinner and rest for the night. Lot obviously had received some good teaching in proper hospitality. That was a big deal in those days.

In the Middle Eastern culture there was a common sense of hospitality, as is evident in the Law of Hammurabi. It was customary in those days (since there wasn't a Motel 6 to leave the light on, as the commercial says) that newcomers, coming into a city, would go to the city square. It was a law that if you saw anyone at the square that was new to the area, you would invite that person to your house for the evening. That wouldn't happen in today's society. Then they would be on their way the next day. If you only had food for two or three people, you were to give food to your guests first. This was a desert setting where food and water were always at a premium. Lot was also bound to the angels by a "water covenant" that occurred when a person gave someone water to drink. This covenant was taken very seriously in their culture. Lot could not just release his guests to an angry mob.

But the consequences of the water covenant wasn't confined to the account of Lot in Sodom. Later in Judges, when Deborah was a judge (leader) of Israel, it came up again. King Jabin of Canaan fought the Israelites through his army, led by general Sisera (Judges 4). The Lord gave Sisera's army into Barak's hand, but General Sisera escaped while all his men were killed (Judges 4:16, 17). He escaped to the tent of Jael, wife of Heber (4:18), who provides him with shelter and milk, but not water (4:19), so she avoided creating a water covenant. She killed him while he slept and when Barak came by, Jael shows him the body. Earlier, Deborah, speaking a prophesy from God (4:9), said that the Lord would HONOR a woman by handing Sisera into her hand. Without his general, King Jaban was eventually destroyed (4:24).

The water covenant is also in the New Testament. When Jesus was going through Sameria, He requested water from the woman at the well (John 4:7). The woman was shocked at His request (4:9) and His disciples, when they returned, were shocked (4:27) as well. It would be unthinkable for a good Jew, especially a Rabbi, to establish a water covenant with a Samaritan, as they were regarded as heretics and corrupters of God's holy Word.

And on the last day of the Feast of Tabernacles (or Booths), when there is much ceremonial pouring of water (the Water Libation Ceremony), Jesus said that He would give Believers streams of Living Water (John 7:37, 38), thus establishing a Water Covenant between mankind and God. So the water covenant can be seen as part and parcel of the plan of salvation; and although this is far away from Lot and the angels in Sodom, it shows that the water covenant is not a minor part of long ago, but a vital part of the Gospel.

These customs had been established prior to the law being given to Moses.

Hospitality was still important to people in Jesus' day. In *Matthew 10:14-15,* Jesus says:

> "If anyone will not welcome you or listen to your words, shake the dust off your feet when you leave that home or town. I tell you the truth; it will be more bearable for Sodom and Gomorrah on the Day of Judgment than for that town."

Jesus was referring to the town of Capernaum. What was the sin of Capernaum? It was the rejection of Jesus Christ and the inhospitality towards His disciples. Jesus says in *Matthew 25:40:*

"The King will reply, 'I tell you the truth, whatever you did for one of the least of these brothers of mine, you did for me.'"

You understand now why the *context* of scripture is important for understanding Sodom and Gomorrah.

Scripture says that two angels informed Lot's Uncle Abraham in Canaan that God was going to destroy all of Sodom because of this evil behavior. That news concerned Abraham because his nephew Lot and Lot's family lived in Sodom. So, Abraham spoke to God and asked, "If I can find fifty righteous in the city of Sodom, would You spare that city?"

That's confidence. It takes a lot of balls to play "Let's Make a Deal" with God. Bargaining with the Creator of the universe in such a fashion is real faith! If nothing else, he was certainty secure in his relationship with God. No "low self-esteem" there!

Abraham bargained with God, and God responded: "If you find fifty, I will spare the city."(*Genesis 18:28*). We can see that God is always willing to look for the good in people and be merciful to humanity. The bargaining continues and goes down to just ten, of which six were Lot and his family. But even at that, God could not find enough righteous people to save the city.

Let me point out something very important about God's message to Abraham. God doesn't tell Abraham what the reason is for the destruction. God does *not* say that it is because of homosexuality. God just says that the city is going to be destroyed. If homosexuality was the reason, then

God would have made a point of sharing that with Abraham. God merely says it is a wicked city.

Eventually, Sodom was destroyed, not because of homosexuality, but because of their general unrighteousness and evil behavior! There are several references to Sodom elsewhere in the Bible, and none of them say that homosexuality was the sin for which God destroyed the city of Sodom:

> "Now this was the sin of your sister Sodom: She and her daughters were arrogant, overfed and unconcerned; they did not help the poor and needy. They were haughty and did detestable things before me. Therefore I did away with them as you have seen." (*Ezekiel 16:49-50*)

There is nothing about homosexuality in there! The city had become indifferent to the widows and orphans, and now to the strangers in their midst. Funds to help the needy, their "social security," so to speak, did not exist. This is part of what God was looking at when He passed judgment on the city of Sodom.

The prophet Isaiah tells us that idolatry, false worship, and injustice were also reasons for the destruction of the two cities, *not homosexuality!*

> "Hear the word of the LORD, you rulers of Sodom; listen to the law of our God, you people of Gomorrah! "The multitude of your sacrifices—what are they to me?" says the LORD. "I have more than enough of burnt offerings, of rams and the fat of fattened animals; I have no pleasure in the blood of bulls and lambs and goats.

When you come to appear before me, who has asked this of you, this trampling of my courts? Stop bringing meaningless offerings! Your incense is detestable to me. New Moons, Sabbaths and convocations—I cannot bear your evil assemblies."

"Your New Moon festivals and your appointed feasts my soul hates. They have become a burden to me; I am weary of bearing them. When you spread out your hands in prayer, I will hide my eyes from you; even if you offer many prayers, I will not listen. Your hands are full of blood; wash and make yourselves clean. Take your evil deeds out of my sight! Stop doing wrong, learn to do right! Seek justice, encourage the oppressed. Defend the cause of the fatherless, plead the case of the widow. 'Come now, let us reason together,' says the LORD. 'Though your sins are like scarlet, they shall be as white as snow; though they are red as crimson, they shall be like wool. If you are willing and obedient, you will eat the best from the land; but if you resist and rebel, you will be devoured by the sword. 'For the mouth of the LORD has spoken." (*Isaiah 1:10-20*)

The big problem in Sodom and Gomorrah was idolatry—worshiping false gods—which is abhorrent to God.

"Do not worship any other gods, for the LORD, whose name is Jealous, is a jealous God." (*Exodus 34:14*)

In *Jeremiah 23:13-14,* we read about false worship and adultery in Israel—things that *heterosexuals* had been doing in Sodom and Gomorrah, and some still practice this today.

"Among the prophets of Samaria I saw this repulsive thing: They prophesied by Baal *(devil worship)* and led my people Israel astray. And among the prophets of Jerusalem I have seen something horrible: They commit adultery and live a lie. They strengthen the hands of evildoers, so that no one turns from his wickedness. They are all like Sodom to me; the people of Jerusalem are like Gomorrah."

Was Israel's degenerate spiritual condition being compared to *homosexuality* in Sodom? Absolutely not! It was being compared to the *paganism, adultery,* and *criminality* in Sodom! These passages are a picture of spiritual wickedness and unfaithfulness in relationships. They reveal false preachers and false prophets. Baal was the god of Sodom, and idolatry was their whole idea of worship. God says that He will have no other Gods before Him. Our God is a jealous God.

It's interesting for me to note that the story of Sodom parallels with the story of Noah. *(Genesis 6:5-8)* Wickedness had been in the land just as it was in Sodom. God destroyed the known earth—which He had created—because of its evil ways. It had nothing to do with destroying the homosexual.

Some fundamentalist preachers still cling to the idea that there was *not one* heterosexual (i.e., righteous) person in the city and that *all* the people of the city of Sodom were homosexuals except Lot and his family. Who is to say that Lot didn't have homosexuals in his own family as well? It seems to me that all extended families have at least one homosexual in them. Remember the statistics? One in ten. Oh my! How can someone be so ignorant? I find it strange that people choose to remain stupid. But ignorance can be cured!

The key verse for using the story of Sodom as anti-homosexual propaganda is Jude 1:7, which in the KJV refers to having "gone after strange flesh." A more convincing interpretation of "strange flesh" would be that (unknowingly) the men (and perhaps the women) of Sodom were attempting to have intercourse with angelic beings. This is something which has received strong approval elsewhere in *Genesis,* and could have been a contributing factor to the Great Flood. (See *Genesis 6:1-4.)* Although it's not entirely clear, but *"the sons of God"* and *"the daughters of men"* could refer to angelic-human crossbreads, called giants (KJV) or Nephilim (NIV). The later use of Nephilim may refer to fully-human giants, like Goliath.

The word translated "giants" or "nephilim" in *Genesis 6* literally means "feller", possibly one who causes another to fall (violently?). This is usually interpreted as a bully or tyrant but could possibly be a fallen one (angel). If so, and if the angelic-human cross-breeds sparked the destruction of the flood, it would seem that human/angelic sexual contact is strongly prohibited.

The word used in *Jude 1:7* is "heteros" (G2087), translated either "strange" flesh (KJV and many others) or "other" flesh (Wycliff, Douay-Rheims). It would seem quite *"unnatural"* to use the word "heteros" to conclude that the subject was homosexual rape. Hetero doesn't usually mean homo.

Now that was a lot of information! So you see that the story of Sodom (and Gomorrah) doesn't really have anything to do with homosexuality, but deals with greed, wrath, cruelty, and inhospitality, just what many gay and lesbian people today suffer at the hands of "good Christian folk" who are in that way imitating "their sister Sodom."

We are seeing more light being shed on these things today as people are coming to terms with their sexuality. Many are admitting that they had become involved in heterosexual marriages only because they wanted to avoid negative repercussions, responses and rejection that they feared would happen if their homosexual feelings were to become known to others. Many of these people are now stepping up, coming *out*, and making things right for themselves and their families, even amidst the difficulty and hurt of coming out as homosexual persons.

I think that many fundamentalists are driven by an anti-gay bias that arose in different places around the world and grew over a long period of time. These fundamentalists, almost no matter where they are, have a tendency to label all gay people the same way. They think that all gay people are out to use and abuse children. But studies and statistics reveal that heterosexual men make up the greatest percentage of the sexual predator population, including the pedophile population. Most child sex trafficking is of underage girls for men. Does this mean that God should punish all heterosexuals? Of course not! Pedophilia is its own thing and is separate from heterosexuality and homosexuality, but some people do not and cannot make that distinction.

Some fundamentalists stereotype gays as being promiscuous and wanting sex without emotional attachments. That stereotype ignores the many long-term and life-long relationships that so many gay people enjoy, and it ignores the desire of so many gay people to solemnize their long-term loving relationships with marriage. Sex addiction classes today are full of heterosexuals who are in bondage to excesses of pornography and promiscuity! Many of these unfortunate people have no concept that loving relationships exist.

Wrong-headed preachers have been saying that big disasters are caused by homosexuality in our country. Not only do they say this about the disaster of Sodom and Gomorroh, they even say it about recent natural disasters! A good example was Hurricane Katrina in 2005. Pat Robertson said that Katrina was God's punishment for homosexuality because it hit the gay-friendly city of New Orleans. But if you look closer, the homosexual area of that city was hardly touched. How can we continue to say that God is judging the world because of its homosexuality? I think it is ignorance! Plain Ignorance! But ignorance can be corrected and cured!

All of this reminds me of the days when the organized church taught that the world was flat. In fact, people were persecuted who taught otherwise. The Church was just following the common misconception of the day and ignored the Bible. God said in *Isaiah 40:20 "God sits enthroned above the circle of the earth."* God knew that the earth was a circle because God had created it as a sphere. God had even shared that information with us in scripture, but most of humanity went blindly past it and didn't realize it.

For centuries the church has persecuted people to justify the enslavement of other people. Preachers once stood in their pulpits and said, "This scripture in the Bible says that we should enslave other people." The truth is, as far as God is concerned, there is ultimately no Jew or Greek, neither black nor white, neither male nor female, gay or straight. We are *all* equal in God's eyes! (*Galatians 3:28*)

There are still those who use the scripture to justify their own *bigotry and hatred* of another people and races. This has got to *stop*! People are killing one another, thinking they are doing God a favor. We need to speak out against this type of injustice. So I am!

Sadly I know of far too many people from the gay and lesbian community who have been put out of their homes and families because of a disagreement over their sexual orientation. I believe that instead of finding the things we don't agree on with each other, we should and need to find the places where we do agree and emphasize them. We should tear down the walls of divisions within families, neighbors, and church families. God hates strife and division. This is what scripture says:

> "There are six things the LORD hates, seven that are detestable to him: haughty eyes, a lying tongue, hands that shed innocent blood, a heart that devises wicked schemes, feet that are quick to rush into evil, a false witness who pours out lies and a person who stirs up conflict in the community." (*Proverbs 6:16-19*)

Today, gay and lesbian Christians are being cast out of some of our Protestant and traditional churches. Openly gay people are not allowed to come into these sanctuaries to hear the Good News, to receive the medicine of the Bible, or to be saved or healed by Jesus the Great Physician. Listening to some preachers today, it sounds like judgment is coming to the world because of homosexuality, not because of the rejection of Jesus Christ.

It should come as no surprise that a great many people in the LGBT community reject Christ because so many "Christians" and "Christian" leaders who compare gay people to the sinners of Sodom and Gomorrah. These churches are turning people away from God's love. Gays are being automatically equated with people described in the Bible who didn't care about others, who were inhospitable to their fellow human beings, who showed excessive pride or arrogance, etc. When gay people transfer that message into their own lives, they feel condemned regardless of how well they try to live their lives. The message of God's acceptance and love for *all* people needs to be expressed from every pulpit in the land.

My message to all LGBT and their allied believers is this:

Any time a statement is made that Sodom and Gomorrah had anything to do with homosexuality, it is a misinterpretation of Scripture. They were cities that refused to help the oppressed, the orphans, the widows, the poor, hungry, and that practiced idolatry. Set this message solidly in your mind: Sodom was *not* destroyed because of homosexuality. Rejoice in that truth!

LGBT Christians please understand that the Bible is *not* against you, it is *for* you! The Bible is actually gay friendly! That will become obvious as we go further.

It has always been clear to me that there are some preachers behind the pulpit that should *not* be there. It is not my job to pass judgment on someone who feels that they are called to be a pastor. However, if they are wrong in this area, isn't it possible that they are wrong in other important areas? No wonder there is so much confusion and division in the church world today!

If you are attending a church looking for spiritual guidance and encouragement, and the person who is speaking for God is giving you an incorrect teaching, then I encourage you to find another place to attend church!

And when a person speaks from ignorance, do they really have the moral right or permission to address this topic when it is so personal and is so damaging to those it excludes from God's grace?

In the United States, we still have the freedom to choose where we want to worship and with whom we want to fellowship. Make sure you are in a church where you can receive correct teaching. The only way to know is to study and know the Bible truths for yourself!

Before you go any further, let me say: if you have been offended or can sense my anger around this issue, and are shocked by any of the information that I have presented so far, you should *stop reading!* It is only going to get worse...or better, depending on your point of view.

I have been watching a lot of RuPaul's Drag Race on the Logo channel and have picked up a new sort of speaking myself, much to the dismay of my family, and even some of my religious friends. Oh, my! I will be using terms and phrases that the people I counsel have used.

I hope that this information is causing joyfulness to rise up in your spirit! Because things are only going to get better as we keep going.

Chapter 6
Rules Is Rules Is Rules...

I'm often reminded of one of my favorite scriptures, *Psalms* 139:14:

"I praise You because I am fearfully and wonderfully made; Your works are wonderful, I know that full well."

As I have mulled over this scripture during my life, the feelings that I had tried to hide became more and more real. How could this scripture *not* be true for an LGBT person living openly in the LGBT community? If I had listened to all of what religiosity says, that would mean that God had made a mistake, and all the gifts and talents that God had given me were null and void. *Numbers* 23:19 says; *"God is not a man that He can lie!"* I knew that *Romans* 11:29 said, *"For God's gifts and His call are irrevocable."* So where did that leave me? I was right in the palm of God's hand where I had always been. It was not a matter of obeying all the rules that my parents and church tried to instill in me, but a matter of understanding God's grace.

My late mother, Helen Electa Birchard/Harvey attended North-Central Bible College in Minneapolis, Minnesota. She had a strong desire to be a part of mission work. For several summers, she and a team of other students traveled to various places in the United States to establish "seed churches" or "Home Mission Churches" for the Assemblies of God. The Assembly of God church in Lewistown, Montana is still in existence today due in large part to her dedication and devotion. She met my father Kenneth, who was killed in a hunting accident in 1973, during one of those crusades in that area. They dated for several months and then married. My mother remained very involved in the church and devoted to missions, but my father was involved only when there was a special occasion.

I was the first born of my family. My spiritual awareness was developed as a child in that same Assembly of God church in Lewistown. My mother wanted to instill in me the heritage of the church through singing hymns. At the Lewistown Assembly, my mother and I would sit towards the back and sing many beautiful hymns. There is one that made me feel accepted while I was trying to deal with my sexuality. It was called Such Love! Such Wondrous Love. The words have always stayed with me, and inspired the title of this book.

> "That God should love a sinner such as I,
> Should yearn to change my sorrow into bliss,
> Nor rest till He had planned to bring me neigh,
> How wonderful is love, like this!
> Such Love, such <u>wondrous love</u>,
> Such Love, such <u>wondrous love</u>,
> That God should love a sinner such as I,
> How wonderful is love like this!"
>
> That for a willful outcast such as I,
> The Father planned the Savior bleed and died;
> Redemption for a worthless slave to buy,
> Who long had law and grace defied.

And now He takes me to His heart a son,
He asks me not to fill a servants place;
"The far off country" wanderings all are done,
Wide open are His arms of Love!
Such Love, such <u>wondrous love</u>,
Such Love, such <u>wondrous love</u>,
That God should love a sinner such as I,
How wonderful is love like this!"
(Robert Harkness & C. Bishop, 1929)

I learned a lot of hymns from my mother as we would harmonize together during the singing portion of the service. When I began to play the organ for the worship portion of the service, I missed singing with her. Later on in life after my father passed, my mother would say; and I started saying: I want him, him, and him! We would laugh at the joke, but I was serious.

It was in Lewistown that I began to learn about Jesus Christ. I had many different Sunday school teachers, Bible teachers, Vacation Bible School teachers, Youth Pastors and Pastors throughout the years. My mother taught "Children's Church." I can still remember her flannel graph stories which made the Bible come alive for me, and her fabulous ability to teach with songs! One children's chorus she taught us went something like this:

Every promise in The Book (Bible) is mine;
Every chapter, every verse, every line.
I am trusting in His love divine.
Every promise in The Book is mine.

I loved that song and still do to this day when sitting around the piano or campfire reminiscing. In contrast to all the wonderful teachings I received, my mother was very strict in her belief about Biblical law and principles.

There are many people who are raised in the "church" who believe that every *law* in the Bible applies to them. I have now discovered that this is incorrect information. Why is it that the laws always apply but the grace doesn't? Do we want just a little grace with some of the law thrown in with it? All of the promises in the Bible are for you and me, but not all of the *laws*. Remember: context!

Many of the Biblical laws have become historical accounts to remind every generation about God's love and provision for His people. Those laws are now open to discussion. Having a more enlightened understanding of scripture in this way does not turn me or others into "theological liberals" or "cultists." We just understand that some portions of scripture were written to guide *specific* individuals or *specific* groups at *specific* times for a *specific* purpose or occasion. That scripture may not have the same relevance to you today.

Let me explain. Did you know that parts of the Old Testament were written only to the ancient nation of Israel? God never intended that they should be applied to 21st century Christians. Probably one of the best examples is the book of *Leviticus*, which has been used to condemn LGBT people down through the ages. Gay Christians often call these "Clobber Passages" because *Leviticus* is one of five main pieces of scripture that have been misinterpreted and mistranslated to condemn homosexuality. These verses are being used against homosexuals to exclude them from many churches and Heaven. *Leviticus* is a clear example of why you must not try to guide your life from a single verse or line in the Bible.

Much of the Old Testament, including *Leviticus,* was written for the Israelites in order to meet the needs of the people in those days. Those stories remind every generation about God's love and provision for His people. When the Israelites entered into the land that God had promised them, God established laws to keep them separate from the existing occupants of the land with their pagan, murderous practices.

In ancient Israel, producing offspring was the most important thing any couple could do to continue the blood line. The mortality rate was very high. Family and heritage depended upon producing children, and the male child was preferred. The Israelites needed to reproduce just to survive as a people.

Single Jewish men were almost non-existent in Israel except in some areas of religious worship. It was customary for every Jewish man to have a wife. The husband didn't have to love his wife; they just had to be married. Often times the parents would choose the spouses for their adult children. The wife then became a possession of the husband. Some cultures still practice this kind of arranged marriage in today's 21st century, if you can imagine that!

It was also expected that every Jewish woman would have children. They were expected to produce at least one male child. If they didn't, they were looked at in disgrace and contempt.

It had been prophesied that the Messiah would come from this select people. That is why Satan has always hated the Jews, and has done everything in his power to destroy them because he knew *that out of the people of Israel* the Messiah would be born. It was part of God's plan to keep the Jewish people intact through the Old Testament period because Jesus Christ was destined to come into this world from among them.

The same need for children is no longer true today. Jewish people live worldwide and have survived some of the worst attacks imaginable to eliminate their existence. Today, statistics show and people realize that heterosexual marriage *is not* for everyone, nor will every heterosexual married person bear children. There are more women in the world today than men, and so it is impossible for everyone to find a life-long mate. In the Old Testament (and also in the Roman Catholic Church) birth control was forbidden. Today we have overpopulated the earth, and birth control is necessary!

In fact, even during some Biblical times, it was recommended that some people remain unmarried and childless. Paul, in his writings to the Corinthians, said that it was good to remain single in those days because Nero at the time was killing Christians right and left.

> "These are troublesome times and it would be better for us to remain single." (*1 Corinthians 7:26*)

This confirms that there is a place for loving relationships that do not produce children.

Moreover, children are not the only gifts we can make to our communities. Childless people and gay people make countless contributions to our society. Look at the beauty in society around you. Much of that is created by gay people.

This includes great artists, musicians, and designers. The list also includes doctors, scientists, teachers, lawyers, and writers. Gay people are in every sector of our society helping to make society better.

In the Old Testament times, the Levitical law was given to the priests of the tribe of Levi. The Levites had to ensure that all of the religious laws were being followed so that they would survive as a people. *Leviticus* is a book of rules written about what was to be eaten, the types of clothing to be worn, a list of sexual restrictions to follow, and a host of other behaviors to be observed. These were to be adhered to by all the children of Israel *in that day*. Here are examples of Levitical laws that no longer apply to us, nor are they to be enforced by our Christian churches

How many of you wear glasses? A lot of you may wear contacts. Well, then, according to the Law of Leviticus, we should be forbidding you from attending services in our churches!

"The LORD said to Moses, "Say to Aaron: 'For the generations to come none of your descendants who have a defect may come near to offer the food of his God. No man who has any defect may come near: no man who is blind or lame, disfigured or deformed; no man with a crippled foot or hand, or who is hunchbacked or dwarfed, or who has *any eye defect*, or who has festering or running sores or damaged testicles. No descendant of Aaron the priest who has any defect is to come near to present the offerings made to the LORD by fire. He has a defect; he must not come near to offer the food of his God. He may eat the most holy food of his God, as well as the holy food; yet because of his defect, he must not go near the curtain or approach the altar, and so desecrate my sanctuary. I am the LORD, who makes them holy." (*Leviticus 21:16-23 (NIV)*)

The above scriptures sound to me like those personal ads that I answered when I began looking to connect with other gay people when I first was coming out! The priests were selecting only the most pleasing or attractive people to the eye.

Tattoos seem to be the popular trend today for both men and women. Do you have a tattoo? Are you a bearded man who trims his beard and sideburns? *Leviticus 19:27-28 NIV* says:

"Do not cut your bodies for the dead or put tattoo marks on yourselves."

"Do not cut the hair at the sides of your head or clip off the edges of your beard."

There are a lot of men with tattoos who get saved later on in life and who involve themselves in various ministries. Yet, these men are accepted into the church. So why is the *homosexual* left out? This is a perfect example of double standards. They follow the law for one person but not the other.

If we were to actually enforce all of Levitical laws today, we would need to start checking people at the front door of the church to make sure that they do not have a tattoo in a place that is covered and are letting their beards and hair grow. So, roll up your sleeves, pull down your pants, and let's feel that fuzz on your chin! How silly is that?

What do you eat for breakfast? *Leviticus 11:6-7* says you may not eat ham or bacon:

"And the pig, though it has a split hoof completely divided, does not chew the cud; it is unclean for you."

Now I know many godly church people with whom I have gone to buffets who pile the bacon onto their plates. They love it! I prefer ham! That makes us sinners because *Leviticus 11:7-8* says,

"Do not partake of these, they are unclean."

A funny open letter appeared on the Internet about ten years ago addressed to Dr. Laura Schlessinger, a radio talk show host who uses *Leviticus* to say that homosexuality is a sin. A couple of the writer's interpretations of *Leviticus* are not exactly correct, but what he says is close enough to make the point with a big dose of humor. I just love it!

"Dear Dr. Laura:

Thank you for doing so much to educate people regarding God's law. I have learned a great deal from your show, and I try to share that knowledge with as many people as I can. When someone tries to defend the homosexual lifestyle, for example, I simply remind him that Leviticus 18:22 clearly states it to be an abomination. End of debate. I do need some advice from you however, regarding some of the specific laws and how best to follow them.

a)   When I burn a bull on the altar as a sacrifice, I know it creates a pleasing odor for the Lord (Lev. 1:9). The problem is my neighbors. They claim the odor is not pleasing to them. Should I smite them?

b)   I would like to sell my daughter into slavery, as sanctioned in Exodus 21:7. In this day and age, what do you think would be a fair price for her?

c)   I know that I am allowed no contact with a woman while she is in her period of menstrual uncleanness. (Lev. 15: 19-24). The problem is, how do I tell? I have tried asking, but most women take offense.

d)   Lev. 25:44 states that I may indeed possess slaves, both male and female, provided they are purchased from neighboring nations. A friend of mine claims that this applies to Mexicans but not Canadians. Can you clarify? Why can't I own Canadians?

e)   A friend of mine feels that even though eating shellfish is an abomination (Lev. 11:10), it is a lesser abomination than homosexuality. I don't agree. Can you settle this?

f)   Lev. 21:20 states that I may not approach the altar of God if I have a defect in my sight. I have to admit that I wear reading glasses. Does my vision have to be 20/20, or is there some wiggle room here?

g) Most of my male friends get their hair trimmed, including the hair around their temples, even though this is expressly forbidden by Lev. 19:27. How should they die?

h) I know from Lev. 11:6-8 that touching the skin of a dead pig makes me unclean, but may I still play football if I wear gloves?

i) My uncle had a farm. He violates Lev. 19:19 by planting two different crops in the same field, as does his wife by wearing garments made of two different kinds of threads (cotton/polyester blend). He also tends to curse and blaspheme a lot. Is it really necessary that we go to all the trouble of getting the whole town together to stone them? (Lev. 24: 10-16) Couldn't we just burn them to death at a private family affair like we do with people who sleep with their in-laws? (Lev. 20:14).

I know you have studied these things extensively, so I am confident you can help. Thank you again for reminding us that God's Word is eternal and unchanging. Your devoted disciple and adoring fan, James M Kauffman, Ed.D. Professor Emeritus, Dept. Of Curriculum, Instruction, and Special Education University of Virginia."

Are you beginning to see how ridiculous it is to apply some Old Testament laws to the 21st century? Apparently many people have not read the portion in *Acts* where Peter is on the roof and when an angel appears to him and commands him to eat *non*-kosher food. This vision is not just about food, dress and other minute restrictions. It means that Christians are no longer bound by all the "laws" that were given to the Israelites to help them during their time of re-integration into society with the peoples around them. Yet, the Christian Right won't let the homosexual person come to church to receive teaching about God because of what they "think" *Leviticus* says about homosexuality. They will not let homosexuals hear of His loving plan for them as homosexuals!

In the Dr. Laura letter, we are reminded of *Leviticus 20:10* which says that if a man commits adultery he is to be taken with the person he committed adultery with and they are both to be killed. When was the last time that you heard a fundamentalist preacher call for everyone in their churches to be killed who had committed adultery? Those preachers surely do know that adultery is being committed by some of the people who are attendees in their churches. Shouldn't those preachers be crying from the pulpits for all adulterers in their congregations to be executed because it says so in *Leviticus*? Some of the preachers themselves may have to be killed! I know several preachers who have fallen in this area of adultery! Yet some of those same fundamentalists are calling for homosexuals to be killed; or at the very least to be put in concentration camps. This just emphasizes the fact that many historical laws cannot be applied to today's society.

Several years ago during a Thanksgiving dinner with my entire family, the subject of homosexuality happened to be brought up. The AIDS epidemic had become a common topic of conversation around the world. During the conversation, my brother—my own flesh and blood—said he thought that all homosexuals should be locked up and put in concentration camps just like the Nazi camps for Jews. I kept silent. I don't remember if I was "out" to my family at that time or not. A gay friend who had come with me to dinner was devastated. Stunned. With all due respect to my brother since I am just using him as one example, that bigoted type of thinking is widespread in the fundamentalist "Christian" churches of this county. The people who want to quarantine homosexuals have a limited understanding of scripture, and either knowingly or unknowingly they are spreading hatred and rejection of the LGBT community in the name of God.

Recently on Facebook, an East coast minister named Rev. Scott Lively and others were advocating that all homosexuals be killed! He is repeating ideas that are widespread in Africa. Recently proposed legislation in Uganda called for all known homosexuals to be executed or jailed for life. This inspired a worldwide outcry, so the legislation was not passed. However, this homicidal idea has vocal support from several evangelical leaders in the United States. The leadership of Exodus International, which is a leading Christian "gay reparative therapy" group, traveled to Uganda along with Michael Brown and some members of Rev. Rick Warren's congregation to support the political agenda of genocide. What? Yes, this is taking place in the 21st century, not in 500 B.C.!

These are but a few of the groups preaching hatred of homosexuality in the name of God. (And I don't even want to talk about what is happening in the Muslim world!) A shocking number of Christians have taken one scripture out of context to prove that homosexuality is punishable by death, while ignoring the other behavioral "sins" that also then should result in death. Jesus came to fulfill the law of grace and love and do away with these restrictions that had been imposed upon an ancient culture. They do not apply to us today!

Many Christians also believe that AIDS is God's punishment of gay people, and that AIDS is their "due penalty for their error." (*Romans 1:27 NIV*). There is nothing "Christian" about that kind of thinking. Where is the love?

Leviticus contains a statement about menstruation that is especially interesting to me because it reveals the hypocrisy of those "Christian" preachers who speak out against the gays. *Leviticus 20:18* says:

> "If a man lies with a woman during her monthly period and has sexual relations [*i.e.*, intercourse] with her, he has exposed the source of her flow, and she has also uncovered it. Both of them must be cut off from their people."

How many heterosexual couples have violated that command? Multitudes would have to be cut off from society. Where would they go? What would they do? Why isn't there a crusade to invade the bedrooms of the heterosexuals for their behavior, like there is for homosexuals? How could you make sure that heterosexual couples are not violating the Levitical law?

Are you seeing how absurd this whole thing is? Come on now! If we are going to do this "Law" thing, then let's do it all the way. The Bible says if you break one part of the Law, you break *all* of the Law.

When I grew up it seemed that everything was a sin! We could not play cards, go to movies, go to teen or high school dances, and girls could not get their ears pierced or wear makeup. Shall I go on? At the same time I knew several people who were always sitting in judgment, pointing things out about "other" people that they felt were wrong. As a pastor I would much rather have people in my congregation who are struggling to do the right thing, than to be around people who are sitting in judgment and pointing out everyone else's flaws while they do not see the flaws in themselves. Those same people who were holy-looking on the outside were ugly, bitter, hateful, intolerable, self-righteous, smug, hypocritical, holier-than-thou, disgusting, and unlovable on the inside. Again, shall I go on? *Luke 6:45* says:

> "A good man (or woman) out of the *good treasure* of his heart bringeth forth that which is good; and an evil man out of the evil treasure of his heart bringeth forth that which is evil: for out of the abundance of the heart his mouth speaketh."

Selective application of Scripture is why many denominations have become legalistic and have negative reputations. How can you reach the lost when you apply *only* those sections of scripture that are comfortable for you? The teachings of the Religious Right are hurting all of us! How is it possible that they can constantly harp on these two small passages from *Leviticus* regarding homosexuality while dismissing entire portions of the same book?

Ignorance! It's just plain ignorance!

In reality, we don't enforce all of these laws because, although they are in scripture, they are not meant for today's world. Remember, all scripture is *for* us, but not all Scripture is *to* us. By that I mean, scripture reminds us of God's love and concern for His people in the past, but the needs of God's people change over time.

Today there is no reason not to cut the hair on the sides of the head even if some orthodox Jewish men still follow that ancient commandment. As Christians, we can respect them for their beliefs without feeling that we need to follow their example.

Let's leave the Old Testament for a moment to look at the New Testament where God makes a *new* covenant with the human race. We read in *Acts 10:9-16:*

> "The next day, as they went on their journey and drew near the city, Peter went up on the housetop to pray, about the sixth hour. Then he became very hungry and wanted to eat; but while they made ready, he fell into a trance and saw heaven opened and an object like a great sheet bound at the four corners, descending to him and let down to the earth. In it were all kinds of four-footed animals of the earth, wild beasts, creeping things, and birds of the air. And a voice came to him, "Rise, Peter; kill and eat." But Peter said, "Not so, Lord! I have never eaten anything common or unclean." A voice spoke to him again the second time, "What God has cleansed you must not call common." This was done three times then the objects were taken up into heaven."

This means that some of the things that God had said were unclean during the days of *Leviticus* were now pro-nounced clean. Even God will change His mind when things change for His people. People can even plead with God and change God's mind as Abraham was able to do in regard to Sodom.

Today's "Religious Right Christian" dismisses 99% of what is written in *Leviticus* and keeps 1% because that 1% touches on same-sex relations. Why is that? They have put God in a box and restricted Him by their narrow understanding of His plans and purposes for humanity.

What are God's *real* plans? *Jeremiah 29:11* reads:

> "For I know the plans I have for you," declares the Lord, "plans to prosper you and not to harm you, plans to give you a hope and a future."

These plans are for *you,* gay or straight!

God's plans call us to responsibility. God doesn't desire that we cheapen our relationships by promiscuity. God's grace doesn't allow us to get away with the anonymous "slam, bam, thank you ma'am" sexual affairs just because other people around us are doing it that way. God calls His people to be at a higher standard. God calls us to responsible living with one another in love.

But there is something else I learned. And it's totally shocking. The 1% of *Leviticus* that some of our Christian friends use to condemn the LGBT community does not even say that homosexuality is against God's plan! It's true! God did not change His mind about homosexuality. God has *always* loved and supported homosexuals! God made us in His own image, after all! This is the next truth I want you to look at. You will be amazed.

Chapter 7
Leviticus Loves You!

Aren't you glad to know that God loves you? Although some of our "Christian" friends would have us believe otherwise, the situations described in the following passages of *Leviticus* are not talking about two guys or gals who have fallen in love with each other, who have set up a home, and are enjoying a loving relationship with mutual respect for one another. Let's look at *Leviticus 18:22* in the NIV: "Do not lie with a man as one lies with a woman; that is detestable."

This passage continues to create havoc in the lives of so many gay Christians today. Obviously men were lying with men or the comparison would not have been made! People were sleeping around with each other even in the Old Testament! Human nature doesn't seem to change too much down through the centuries of time!

I will try to keep this as clinical as possible, but I have to admit I would like to use gutter terms if just for the shock value. When *Leviticus* states that men should not have intercourse with men *"as with a woman,"* some people think it means that men should not have intercourse with each other in the same *manner* that they would have intercourse with women. That would mean that the act of a male penetrating into the anal canal of another male, *i.e.,* having sex in a manner similar to heterosexual intercourse, is incorrect and sinful.

This would have made sense from a health perspective in those days. Anal intercourse can cause rectal bleeding for people who don't practice anal intercourse correctly. Bleeding and open sores can bring infection. In Old Testament times before there was any such thing as antibiotics, such wounds could be fatal. This does not mean that other forms of homosexual expression could not be practiced, like oral stimulation! Maybe that's what President Clinton meant when he said he didn't have sex with Monica Lewinski! I told you I would be keeping these topics real! A later verse of *Leviticus* (20:13) seems to repeat 18:22:

"If a man lies with a man as one lies with a woman, both of them have done what is detestable. They must be put to death; their blood will be on their own heads."

Some people say that this bit of *Leviticus* actually refers to rape after a victory in battle. If you use the resources I recommended earlier, and match the words in *Leviticus* to the original Hebrew words, we might get this:

"If a man [Strong's #376: 'îysh] *has intercourse* [Strong's #7901: shâkab] *with a man* [Strong's #2145: zâkâr] *as with a woman* [Strong's #802: 'ishshâh], *both commit an abomination* [Strong's #8441: tôw'êbâh]."

Rape in battle occurred when one tribe defeated another tribe. The losers were taken into slavery and raped for humiliation as one of the "rights" of victors to humiliate a defeated people.

This is why King Saul, who was wounded in a battle, was afraid that he would be raped as a prisoner. Before his death he asked his son Jonathon to kill him so he wouldn't have to endure that humiliation. Jonathan wouldn't do it, and, Saul took his own life because he did not want to be "abused" by the uncircumcised enemy.

But notice in *Leviticus* 20:13 that the Hebrew word for the first "man" ('îysh) is different than the word used for the second "man" *(zâkâr)*. Both those Hebrew words were mistakenly translated into English as simply "man" as though they meant the same thing. But they don't mean the same thing! The first "man" is correctly translated as the generic "man," but the second "man" is *zâkâr* which denotes a male who is "noteworthy," such as a king or man of the temple.

Looking further at the sentence, the Hebrew word translated as "woman" *('ishshâh)* was commonly used to mean "adulteress." The Hebrew word translated as "abomination" *(tôw'êbâh)* commonly meant "idolatry,' *i.e.,* forbidden worship.

So what did this passage from *Leviticus really* say was forbidden? The best English translation of *Leviticus 20:13* seems to be, *"If a man commits adultery with a temple male, both commit idolatry."* The offense is temple prostitution, not homosexuality.

When *Leviticus* was written, some Gentile fertility cults in the region offered sex with priests or young male prostitutes. The "noteworthy" men of *Leviticus* were probably those priests and prostitutes. Jewish law prohibited the Jews from consorting with such people in the pagan temples because it would constitute a form of adultery (sex outside of marriage) and idolatrous worship.

We are lucky that we have the tools today to discover this true meaning and understand God's actual Word so that we can have a better relationship with Him. It helps us to break down the ignorance and wrong "traditions" of past human thinking. I told you ignorance can be cured! Again, let me encourage you to make use of the resources that I have mentioned for your own personal Bible study.

God knew that as soon as the Israelites settled into the land of Canaan after forty years of wandering, they would mingle with their new neighbors who practiced pagan religions and worshiped many gods, not the one true God of the Israelites. Some of the commands in the Levitical Law were designed to prevent the Israelites from committing pagan acts, one of which was the act of ceremonial sex.

The Canaanites believed that the fertility of their crops and livestock, and their own ability to have children, would be guaranteed by an act of sexual union between them and the god Baal or the goddess Ashtoreth through the temple priests, priestesses, and prostitutes. So for a farmer to do his fair share, he would participate in ceremonial sexual intercourse for which he would pay a tithe that would help support the temple. No wonder the cult houses of worship were so popular! They provided a place for men to get their "jollies" with an excuse that it was "religious."

Why *male* prostitutes? Male prostitutes were popular because they couldn't get pregnant. No doubt the worshipers timed their temple visits to coincide with the most gorgeous "hotties" of the day! I know I would have!

Many pagans did believe in the spiritual rationale for ceremonial sex. It seemed reasonable to them in that day and age. They thought that this kind of physical contact would also push away the bad spirits that they believed were hindering successes in life. Sexual intercourse was considered to be an effective way to gain the favor of the gods and goddesses.

The Levites realized that these temple practices did not support the style of worship that was glorifying to Jehovah, their one and only God. The sexual practices were a form of idolatry. We also know that in the male anatomy, the big head often follows the urgings of the little head. That is why God had to set such stringent rules for men to have sexual relations only with their partners and stay away from the temple prostitutes.

The Bible does not deal with sexual *orientation*, but with a person's sexual *behavior*. So with a clear conscience you gay and lesbian people can set these pieces of Levitical scripture aside when discussing homosexual orientation and acceptability to God. It's not who you have interpersonal relationship with; it is how that intimacy is experienced and expressed. Please get that concept solid, secure, firmly fixed, assured and accepted in your spirit! It will help you in understanding everything you read in regards to being gay and Christian.

Ask yourself these questions:

Do you practice paganism? No.

Do you worship idols? No.

Do you rape people? Hopefully not.

Then you don't fit into the *Leviticus* ban! Period!

Keep that in mind because it is so helpful to reading the entire Bible in context.

So why are the homosexuals singled out by misinterpreting *Leviticus?* After all, it is really the heterosexuals who need most of our attention. The Bible says much more about heterosexual behavior than it does the behavior of homosexuals. As a matter of fact, there are hundreds of passages admonishing heterosexual couples on how they are to live. Only five scriptures seem to refer to homosexuals. Isn't that an interesting fact?

I believe that many well-meaning Christians are sincere in their traditional thinking when they say they want gays to "get right with God" and not miss out on Heaven. Although they fail to really understand that Christianity for the LGBT persons is not based on our homosexual orientation but on Jesus Christ and what He did for *all* humanity on the cross thousands of years ago! Some "well-meaning Christians" misrepresent the scriptures and badger the LGBT community with the very book that was written to bring freedom and redemption to everyone.

If you believe in *total* redemption through Jesus and what Jesus has already done on the cross, then there is nothing you can do to lose your salvation or make it any better! Hallelujah! Amen!

One of the crazy ways that Christian fundamentalists "prove" that homosexuality is against God's will is to point to behaviors that violate the Word or accepted standards of modern-day society. They have made documentaries about gay people who go to bathhouses, use drugs, or are convicted of pedophilia, to imply that such behavior is the "gay lifestyle."

What is silly about that is we can make a documentary about heterosexuals in the same way. We can show pictures of brothels in Nevada, of "swinger clubs" and "wife swapping" ads, and of the many heterosexuals who use drugs.

Such behavior is rampant! We could put all of this together into a documentary about the "sick heterosexual lifestyle" and demand that heterosexuals be banned from the churches. Homosexuals don't make such accusations or documentaries because they realize how ridiculous it all is.

My mother was still alive when I founded and now am the senior pastor of an LGBT congregation. She actually thought we were performing some sort of sexual activities in our gay Christian worship services! When I tried to explain that it wasn't true, her attitude was, "Don't tell me anything different. My mind is already made up! I won't believe you anyway." She even came to one of our renewal weekends. She still didn't want to believe homosexuals could be gay and Christian! This is because of her church traditions, and this is what is being preached from many of the pulpits in some conventional churches. It's like trying to put new information or revelation into old ways of thinking. You can't put new wine in old wineskins! If she had been correct, then my Sunday worship services would have been packed. In fact, my congregation worships just a few blocks away from a very popular gay bath house here in San Jose. But *our* idea of "hot action" is a potluck with hot foods!

I am sorry to say, but my mother told me on numerous occasions that I am going to hell for the lifestyle I have chosen. Lifestyle? Chosen? Who in their right mind would choose this lifestyle? Do I want to be despised and ridiculed by my friends, family and loved ones? Do I want to be discriminated against in my job, the place I live, etc.? *No!* Where is the common sense and Christian love in those sorts of statements? The Scripture says that those who judge their brothers are guilty of the same thing. Where is the "judge not lest you be judged"? These thoughts still resonate in my heart today! In my head I know that my mother's words were not true, but my heart still feels the wounds of those words.

For most gay couples, the "gay lifestyle" is exactly like the "straight lifestyle." Gays are fighting for the right to marry so that they can live that equal lifestyle. Homosexuals experience the same emotions as heterosexuals when their relationships succeed or fail. Most gay people are just as concerned about love and commitment in their relationships as straight people are in theirs. A popular joke is that gays should be allowed to marry so that they can suffer just like straights. A comedy video starring Justin Long came out in 2010 for the so-called "Make Gays Marry Campaign." The video shows what can happen to many gay couples after being together a long time. They fall into the same boring routines and lead the same dull lives as many heterosexual couples…but it's not routine and dull as long as there is love.

The Bible says *knowledge* will increase in the Last Days before the coming of Jesus Christ. Remember that in 1973, homosexuality was declassified as a mental illness. This occurred because of developments in the science of psychology and new understandings about brain development. *I thought you might need to be reminded of that!*

I quote from an article that Father Geoffrey Farrow wrote in the October 5, 2008 *San Jose Mercury News*. I feel he said it well when he addressed the Catholic bishops in California:

> "In directing the faithful to vote "Yes" on Proposition 8 [the California anti-gay marriage initiative], the California Bishops are not merely entering the political

arena, they are ignoring the advances and insights of neurology, psychology and the very statements made by the Church itself that homosexuality is innate. In doing this, they are making a statement which has a direct, and damaging, effect on some of the people who may be sitting in the pews next to you today. The statement made by the bishop reaffirms the feelings of exclusion and alienation that are suffered by individuals and their loved ones who have left the Church over this very issue. Imagine what hearing such damaging words at Mass did to an adolescent who had just discovered that he/she is gay/lesbian?"

How did you feel or know someone who felt, when you saw a car with a "Yes on 8" bumper sticker? How did you feel when you overheard someone in a public place use the word "faggot?"

Now pause. Think. What would those words mean to someone in junior high school who discovers that he/she is attracted to people of the same gender? The greatest fear that such people would have is that they would be rejected by the people they love the most—their family. So, their solution is to try to pass as straight, to deceive, and in effect—to lie. Of course, this leads ultimately to self-loathing. It should come as little surprise that gay teenagers have elevated suicide rates. According to the Center for Disease Control's Youth Risk Behavior Survey (1999), 33% of gay youth will attempt suicide.

So now we must ask ourselves why some Christians are trying to force LGBT people into the dark places by making them feel like they need to stay hidden? It is the dark places where people can still be exploited, like the back alleys where drugs, promiscuity, disease and death still occur. Our Christian friends do not see that this is why there is so much confusion and hurt around this subject of homosexuality. Everyone, gay and straight, needs to be encouraged to stay in the Light! When people are cut off from where the Light is, the sinful thoughts begin that eventually turn into actions.

Now again, before you get too offended, let me clear up what I mean by our "Christian" friends. It is my opinion that there are true Christians and there are false Christians in every denomination in America. Their character is what sets them apart. If our "Christian" friends are not operating in love, then they are immature Christians. This is what I refer to as false Christians.

At this point, you might still be asking yourself, what does *Leviticus* mean by "abomination"? It is important to clear up the misunderstandings about this word once and for all.

Chapter 8
What's Up With Abomination?

꿍

We need to talk about the word "abomination." Some people have become so confused that they think "abomination" and "homosexuality" mean almost the same thing. They don't. Not even close.

Most people seem to think that "abomination" means "something terrible." But in the Old Testament, the word was taken from the Hebrew *ebah* which is the equivalent for *idolatry* or *idol worship*. God hates idolatry and states that He won't share His glory with anyone! This was true when *Leviticus* was written, and it is still true today.

> "You shall not worship them or serve them; for I, the LORD your God, am a jealous God..." *(Exodus 20:5)*

> "...for you shall not worship any other god, for the LORD, whose name is Jealous, is a jealous God." *(Exodus 34:14)*

In Latin, abomination is *abominatus*, past participle of *abominari*, which means "to deprecate as an ill omen." Even in Latin, the word still has that connection to pagan practices.

Homosexuality was considered wrong when it was practiced in connection with pagan temple prostitution, because then it was connected to idolatry in the minds of the Jewish people of Old Testament times. Heterosexuality was every bit as big a sin when it was practiced as idolatry! It wasn't the homosexuality or heterosexuality that was wrong; it was using *any kind* of ceremonial sex for idolatrous worship.

The Bible says nothing negative about same-gender loving committed relationships and lifestyles. We will see, in fact, that it encourages them just as much as it glorifies opposite-gender loving committed relationships! The only prohibitions were about cultic worship and use of sex for humiliation.

During the course of history, these passages became mistranslated because of bias and misunderstanding. The wrong conclusions were reached that all homosexuality is evil, pagan, and against the nature of God when that is *not* what God was telling us through the prophets.

If Jesus were here on Earth today, I believe He would go to those who are saying such things, and just like Margaret Cho in her dialog on "Those Christian Groups Have Lost Their Minds," tap them on the shoulder, look them in the eye, shake them really hard and say, "I never meant it that way!"

I have also found that those who call homosexuality an "abomination" try to "prove" their cause by finding every scripture they can pertaining to sexual sin and promiscuity. It is important to understand that we Christians in the gay community are also against sexual sin. The difference lies in the fact that we do not believe God has singled out any particular community or nation of people as "evil" or 'sinful'. We believe instead that God's statutes are applied without prejudice to all peoples and communities; homosexual and heterosexual alike.

Therefore before calling homosexuality a sin, one should cross—reference Scripture to find if this premise is even true. Unfortunately, many "well-meaning Christians" are just repeating what they have heard from the pulpit and are attempting to frame God's will around their own prejudices and fears.

We have examined the word "abomination" in the Old Testament. What about in the New Testament? *Vines Expository Dictionary* provides the following definitions of the Greek words:

As an adjective: from the root *Athemitos*: It means unlawful.

As a verb: *Edelukotos*, meaning abhor.

As a noun: *Edelugma,* meaning an object of disgust, and is used in scripture to identify the idolatrous image that will be set up by the Antichrist.

The association of these words with idolatry suggests that what is highly esteemed among men can sometimes constitute an idol in the human heart. We see again that "abomination" is a synonym for "idolatry."

The prophets of the New Testament were like the prophets of the Old Testament. They continually and repeatedly warned God's people against idolatry. I'm going to give you an example of an especially detestable idolatrous practice to emphasize this point. It was the offering of babies and young children to the pagan god Molech, who was the pagan fire god.

Followers of Molech believed that their idols could only be appeased by offering tiny children into the fires that continually burned in their honor. Idolaters would offer their first born. The God of Israel said to the Jewish people that the first born males were to be dedicated to Him. They were to be raised as priests and dedicated to God's service.

2 Kings 23:10 provides a description of Molech worship and how God warned the people of Israel, as they intermingled with the pagans around them, not to be a part of this practice because it was an abomination (idolatrous) and detestable. Molech worshippers were preforming idolatry in its worst form. That's why *Leviticus 18:21* specifically forbade it:

"Do not give any of your children to be sacrificed to Molech, for you must not profane the name of your God. I am the LORD."

This verse comes just before the verse about lying with a man as with a woman. This is further proof that the ban is about pagan worship, not homosexuality. Isn't that interesting? Remember God was instructing the Israelites to remain separate from the pagan practices that they were being exposed to in the Promised Land.

Incidentally, this is why *Leviticus 20:1-5* also banned tattoos. Molech cultists practiced painting their bodies to resemble the flames of fire. *Leviticus* said that God's people were not permitted to enter the true sanctuary of God if they had images etched into their bodies. In other words, tattoos were associated with idolatry. Today, most people don't get tattoos for idolatrous purposes, and so we don't enforce *Leviticus 20:1-5* in our Christian churches.

With the passing of time, even many of the pagans became offended by the baby slaughter. They decided that Molech could be appeased by offering male sperm. Rather than offering children, male sperm was placed in the fire instead of babies. Some of the men of Israel were entertained by masturbating in this way and started joining in. This was an "abomination" to God not because the men were involved in social masturbation, but because it was done as part of an idolatrous practice. To put it crudely, if men are circle-jerking together without any religious attachment to it, there is nothing in the Bible that says it is wrong unless it is being done by someone who is already in a relationship. (I told you not to read this book if this kind of talk offends or upsets you!)

Sexual orientation really boils down to whom we are drawn to share our love with in a romantic sense. How do we know someone is in love today? There will be gifts, phone calls, emails and spending time together. The main and ultimate display of love is when the companionship is public, like being seen together at family reunions and dinners, or at get-togethers with friends or office parties. That's how you know it is real love, not just a temporary sexual connection.

I say the same things apply to our relationship with God. When you love God, you're going to talk to Him, and you can't wait to talk to Him. You'll talk to Him in your car, when you are preparing food, getting ready for bed, and when you get up in the morning. You talk *about* Him all the time.

If you love the Lord, you are going to read His love letter to you, which is the Bible. You may read it through quickly the first time. The second time you will read it a little slower. Then the third or fourth time you are going to take a pencil and underline the good parts. I think when you really love the Lord, you are going to introduce Him to people and let everyone know how important He is to you. You will desire to bring your friends and family to church to meet your spiritual family. This is the kind of love that God desires for us to experience with Him…and with each other!

This kind of love is *not* an "abomination" in any sense of the word. If you call it an "abomination" when it is between people, gay or straight, then you will have to call it an abomination when it is experienced with God. Love is God's most wonderful gift to us, something to be shared in our relationships with each other and in our relationship with Him.

As we have seen, there is nothing about homosexuality that is an abomination. Only when sexual activity is part of idol worship does it become an abomination. There's nothing wrong with unconditionally loving your spouse, your partner, your friends, and your church family. It is in learning to love others that we also learn to love ourselves as the men and women that God has created.

You may be asking right now, what about the word "fornication"? It sounds kind of similar to "abomination." Isn't gay sex, by definition, "fornication?"

"Fornication" usually means sex outside of marriage, but since gays are not allowed to marry in most places, some people call it "fornication." This is the reason why a few people believe it is OK to be gay as long as they remain celibate.

The word "fornication" does not even come to my mind when I think of gay sex. I think of people in committed relationships as being "married" whether or not it has been recognized with a secular marriage license. In the Bible, "fornication" also refers to sex in connection with idolatry.

Fornication becomes a stumbling block for some Christians, especially those that I have spoken to in the Roman Catholic tradition. There is a passage in the New Testament where Jesus says that looking upon a woman with lust in your heart is the same as having committed adultery with her. *(Matthew 5:28)* This text has sometimes been used as a justification for an unrealistic and extreme attitude toward sexuality.

Such an attitude actually attempts to destroy sexual feelings in the name of righteousness, totally ignoring the endorsement of sexuality found in other parts of the Bible such as in *Song of Solomon*. Young men within the Roman Catholic Church are taught that they have committed a mortal sin (a sin that will ultimately put them in Hell) if they indulge themselves by letting themselves feel desire for an attractive person, male or female. How can one possibly avoid being a "sinner" with this type of legalism?

The New Testament never speaks about particular acts of sex. However you choose to pleasure your mate is your business. The Bible says that the marriage bed is to be kept pure. *(Hebrews 13:4)* It talks about sex as it relates to marriage/commitment. I believe there is a reason for this: God cares about the heart. If your heart is healthy and holy, then your sexual expression will follow suit. A helpful study on this topic can be found at http://www.gaychristian.net/greatdebate.php.

I think the best proof that loving homosexual relationships are not an "abomination" or "fornication" to God are the same-gender relationships in the Bible. While we have no definitive proof that such relationships were actually sexual, I believe that some of them were, and it is inspiring to ponder this.

Chapter 9
Who's Gay In The Bible? Inquiring Minds Want To Know

Many writers today have endeavored to show that there were homosexual relationships in the Bible. Is there truth to this idea, or are they grasping at straws? I wasn't there, so of course I can't say for sure. But I do know that as long as the relationships did not involve idolatry, and were based on love and loyalty, they would have been perfectly fine with God.

I know that you might be resistant to the idea that any homosexual relationships existed in scripture due to the homophobic teaching that has come forth on this topic. I'm asking you to set aside any prejudices and preconceived notions, and consider with me that we have not been taught all that God would have us know on this topic.

Science has shown that ten percent of the male population, and five to six percent of the female population, is homosexual. What makes anyone think that it was any different back in Biblical days? That means that ten percent of the men, and five to six percent of the women, in the Bible were gay. So, what's the big deal if we ask:

Were Ruth and Naomi lesbians?

Were Jonathan and David lovers?

What about Elijah and Elisha?

Or Daniel and Ashpenaz?

Was the apostle Paul a latent (closeted) homosexual?

And the most shocking question of all, were John and Jesus lovers?

Let's try to shed some light on these questions. Don't run away. Wait and see what I am about to tell you.

Ruth and Naomi

Were Ruth and Naomi lesbians? Many of you lesbians reading this may have suspected or hoped for it.

The Bible never mentions any physical relations between the two women. It does say that they had a very close emotional bond. They had been thrown together by family circumstances.

Ruth was married to one of Naomi's sons, but he died. Ruth was a Gentile. Naomi was a Jew. Ruth became devoted to her mother-in-law Naomi. By adopting Naomi's homeland and family as her own, Ruth became part of the line through which the Messiah was eventually to be born as the result of Ruth's marriage to her second husband, Boaz. What a privilege!

The story of Ruth and Naomi is a wonderful account of a deep, abiding friendship—even love—that developed between a mother and her daughter-in-law in a very difficult situation.

In that time, a woman without a man had no social standing. No one was there to take care of her. The sensible thing would have been for Ruth to return to her family after her first husband died, but instead she chose to stay with Naomi. This decision was based on one word: love. The story had nothing to do with an intimate sexual relationship as far as we know, although it would have been fine if it did have sexual implications. On the other hand, their actions and emotions are very difficult to explain as mere friendship; it is more like the companionship between spouses. We might call this "homo-affection" rather than "homosexuality."

The two women made vows, this mysterious pledge to each other that are still used in wedding ceremonies today: *"Where you go I will go, and where you lodge I will lodge. Your people shall be my people, and your God shall be my God."* They lived together, loved each other deeply, Ruth adopted Naomi's extended family, and relied on each other for sustenance and support as do many lesbian couples today. They remained together until Naomi died. The Bible celebrates their relationship by giving them their own book in the Bible. To me there are many degrees of love and affection. This is definitely shown in the book of Ruth.

Jonathan and David

If there is any record of homosexual love in the Bible, it is most likely between Jonathan and David. Their relationship is possibly the most moving love story in the entire Bible. David and Jonathan are presented in a very positive light, and their feelings for each other give many hints at a sexual relationship.

In *1 Samuel* we are told how God chose, though the prophet Samuel, a young man named David to become the next king of Israel. God is all-knowing and would have known David's sexual preferences, and thus would not have been displeased if David was gay.

Jonathan, meanwhile, was the son of King Saul.

1 Samuel 16:12 describes David as ruddy with a fine appearance and possessed of handsome features. The Bible says that when Jonathan first saw David, he was immediately drawn to David's good looks. Jonathan's heart evidently did flip-flops. It was love at first sight. We all know those feelings. The fact that the Bible goes to the trouble of telling us about David's handsomeness says something about the nature of Jonathan's attraction to him. It was very rare for the Bible to talk about people's physical features, and it seems to happen mostly when there was a good-looking possibly-gay "hottie" like David, Daniel or Timothy. You may see this as silliness from a gay person, but look in the Bible and read for yourself.

The first meeting between David and Jonathan is described in *1 Samuel 18:1-3 NIV:*

> "After David had finished talking with Saul, Jonathan became one in spirit with David, and he loved him as himself. From that day Saul kept David with him and did not let him return to his father's house. And Jonathan made a covenant with David because he loved him as himself."

Let's analyze that passage. The following original Hebrew words are translated literally in order that we can arrive at an accurate meaning. (Numbers indicate references in Strong's dictionary):

...Jonathan (#3083) [was] knitted (or "closely joined") (#7194) [by] bodily desire (#5315) [to] David (#1732) [and] affection (#157); [for] Jonathan (#3083) [David] felt bodily desire (#5315)....Cut [between] (#3772) Jonathan (#3083) [and] David (#1732) [was] a covenant (#1285) [of] love (#160) [and] bodily desire (#5315).

Most of us enjoy being romantic. However, the strong desire of men for a more visual eroticism is well known. Let's face it; it's men who mostly patronize strip clubs and topless bars. Men have a strong visual appreciation for the beauty of the human body. Gay men can appreciate the very loving and emotionally powerful relationship between Jonathan and David:

"Jonathan took off the robe he was wearing and gave it to David, along with his tunic and even his sword, his bow and his belt." *(I Samuel 18:4)*

Jonathan stripped naked! His act of disrobing for David reinforces the idea of a sexual relationship. The things that Jonathan gave David represented power, position, royalty, and military might. Jonathan was willing to share it all with David. Why was he so generous? It was because he was completely smitten with David and loved David with all that was within him.

I Samuel 19 says that Jonathan "delighted in David." And, I might add, it is obvious that David delighted in Jonathan! After another secret meeting between Jonathan and David, we read in *1 Samuel 20:41:*

"...David got up from the south side of the stone and bowed down before Jonathan three times, with his face to the ground. Then they kissed each other (on the lips) and wept together—but David wept the most."

Sounds like something I would do! I cry, too, whenever I am going to be apart from someone for an unknown amount of time!

In the *Deuey Rheims Roman Catholic* translation of the 1600s, King Saul calls Jonathan *"a ravisher of a man"*! *Deuey Rheims* also translates *I Samuel 20:41* to say that David and Jonathan "kissed one another until David exceeded." The phrase "one another" comes from the Hebrew *iysh reya* in which *iysh* means "male" and *reya* means "with male lover." "Exceeded" in Hebrew is *gadal. Gadal* means "lifted up, grew up, enlarged." In other words, it sounds like David got an erection and had an organism kissing Jonathan.

In *1 Samuel 18:21*, Saul gives one of his daughters to David in marriage for the first time and says to David, "... you shall now be my son-in-law." This doesn't sound at all controversial, but in the NRSV there is a footnote that the actual Hebrew phrase is "you shall now be my son-in-law *by two*." This sounds like David was married to two of Saul's adult children, but he was only married to *one* of Saul's *daughters*. Was the other child *Jonathan*?? Does the Bible actually have a gay marriage in it—a marriage blessed by God? (Remember that Jewish men at the time often had multiple spouses.)

To get around this "problem," the NRSV just deletes the "by two." The King James Version inserts the extra words "one of," thereby making the verse read: "...you shall now be my son-in-law by one of the two," which implies one of Saul's two *daughters*. Both translations seem to purposely avoid any possibility of a homosexual connotation. But if we stick to the actual Hebrew text: "…you shall now be my son-in-law by two," it can be seen as affirming that David would be the son- in-law by both Jonathan and Jonathan's sister Michal.

Just like many LGBT people today, Jonathan and David encountered extreme opposition to their relationship from at least one of their parents, at least for a while. In this case, that opposition eventually came from Jonathan's father King Saul. Look *at 1 Samuel 20:1-3:*

> Then David fled from Naioth at Ramah and went to Jonathan and asked, "What have I done? What is my crime? How have I wronged your father that he is try-ing to take my life?" "Never," Jonathan replied. "You are not going to die! Look, my father doesn't do anything, great or small, without confiding in me. Why would he hide this from me? It's not so!" But David took an oath and said, "Your father knows very well that I have found favor in your eyes, and he has said to himself, 'Jonathan must not know this or he will be grieved.' Yet as surely as the LORD lives and as you live, there is only a step between me and death."

Did you notice that sentence where it says, "Your father knows that you have found favor in my eyes"?

There is more. *1 Samuel 20:17* tells us:

> So Jonathan made a covenant with the house of David saying, "May the Lord God call David's enemies to re-

count." And Jonathan had David reaffirm his oath out of love for him, because he loved him as he loved himself."

And that's not all.

"Saul's anger flared up at Jonathan and he said to him, "You son of a perverse and rebellious woman! Don't I know that you have sided with the son of Jesse to your own shame and to the shame of the mother who bore you?" (*1 Samuel 20:30*)

How many times have our mothers had to bear the brunt of embarrassment from their church families because of accusations made that their children were homosexual? At my mother's funeral, I learned from the comments of various parishioners that people at her Assembly of God church knew I was gay. I am sure she would have been humiliated since this is not acceptable in their belief system. I learned that at their weekly prayer meetings, my mother would always request a prayer that I would not miss out on Heaven. These people more than likely didn't even know me, but my mother felt she needed to share this information so that the people of God could pray more effectively. It became obvious to me that she had expressed doubts to many people about my making it to Heaven because of my homosexuality! When I heard these comments at her funeral, I was shocked and hurt. I had been "outed" to people who didn't even know me. And I also noticed that I was not referred to as a pastor or reverend in her funeral bulletin. More than likely it was because the people from her church knew I was gay.

Later in the service, I sang the song she had requested that I sing at her funeral. When I got up to sing, I took a deep breath and responded to their concerns about my eternal destination. *"Yes!"* I said with confidence. *"All* of Helen's children will one day be in Heaven with her!" I still well up with emotion when I remember how badly her doubts were handled by her church. Mother was just so sure that I was being deceived and I was going to Hell that she needed to constantly ask in prayer for my salvation! She also used to send me birthday cards telling me how I needed to change my life so that I wouldn't miss Heaven. It put a distance between us. Then she would call me a week later like everything was normal and fine. She never considered how hurtful her words were, and how deeply they pierced my heart. God had called me to minister for Him, and my life was dedicated to serving Him, yet my mother couldn't see beyond the prejudicial traditional church teachings.

Despite her "Happy Birthday, but You're Going to Hell" cards, I know her heart was in the right place. When God heard her prayers, He knew her intentions were for my good, so He interpreted them in a way that was good for all concerned! So many sincere people that I know personally are afraid to question what they have been taught for generations by their parents, teachers, and childhood preachers because they are afraid it will endanger their eternal salvations! My mother clung to those old teachings and limited learning, and sadly, was not able to accept any new insights that the Holy Spirit has been giving to this generation. I had presented new information to her on numerous occasions.

Her heart and mind were set even though I was "called and anointed" as a minister of the Gospel! *(Romans 11:29 NIV)* And yet she would wonder how I could be so rebellious and blind. But, I know that when my mother arrived at the pearly courts of Heaven, she got all the misinformation corrected. Now she knows that I am accepted by God and I will be with her one day. Bless His holy wonderful name forever!

I digressed, but I had to take a moment. Let's get back to the subject at hand...

In *1 Samuel*, chapter 20, when Saul threw a spear at his son Jonathan and called him the son of a perverse woman, he was saying "like mother, like son." Maybe Jonathan really wanted to be "queen," and his father Saul knew it! That's what I think. Elsewhere in *1 Samuel*, Jonathan tells David that King Saul knew that Jonathan would be next to David (on the throne), which would mean David as king and Jonathan as his queen! Oh my! There's just so much drama!

Tragically, Jonathan and his father Saul died in battle. David expressed his deep love afterwards. *2 Samuel 1:26* shares his moving words:

"I grieve for you, Jonathan my brother; you were very dear to me. Your love for me was wonderful, more wonderful than that of women."

If people today were behaving like David and Jonathan, we would say, "That's so gay." We would most certainly tag them as gays, or at least as bisexuals.

All of this inspired scripture gives David and Jonathan's love a positive tone. The intimate and sexual meanings behind the words appear in early Hebrew text but were omitted in the Greek translation.

David went for months grieving over Jonathan's death. Yet we often hear the story of David and the woman Bathsheba, and how David desired her beauty and had her husband murdered so that he could be with her. This all occurred *after* the death of Jonathan. This lends credence to David and Jonathan's love affair. Because he could not have Jonathan, David seems to have gotten crazy and lost perspective. In his grief he seems to have been looking for someone to fill the void of Jonathan. He seemed to behave like many Christian gay people today when they suffer the loss of their Christian or church families. Because they have been deprived of those relationships, they may go out and engage in risky behavior trying to fill that painful void. They may have sex with numerous people that they may or may not even know. Thus they take a chance on getting a disease. And that's what finally happened to David.

Some people believe that King David died from a sexually transmitted disease: syphillis. What? You have never heard of this? Well, I'm not making it up! Reputable scholars have developed this theory based on sound research. Most people don't recognize the symptoms of syphillis, which was especially true in that day, and they would hardly attribute such a disease to King David being that he was *a man after God's own heart*. After Jonathan died, King David had sex where he shouldn't have.

But didn't David also have many traditional wives and concubines? Isn't that also true of Jonathan? Doesn't that "prove" that they were heterosexual after all? Absolutely not! As a king, it was expected of David. King David had to marry and have children for political and social reasons. He had many wives, as did his son King Solomon who had seven hundred in order to keep peace in the empire and with the surrounding populations. The family connection created by each marriage meant one less ruling family against whom one might need to wage war. It also meant more influence.

Even though David and Jonathan both had wives, we know that their deepest love was for each other. How many spouses today are caught having same-sex affairs outside their heterosexual marriages? Just read the headlines when these affairs are exposed. I don't need to make a list for you. You get the point. How sad that in this century those people still feel forced to live a lie.

The story of David and Jonathan might help us to understand the passages in the next book of the Bible, *Ecclesiastics*. *Ecclesiastics* was written by King Solomon, who was David's son.

In *Ecclesiastics 4:9-11*, we read that men who share a life and bed together are totally OK with God:

> "Two are better than one, because they have a good return for their work: If one falls down, his friend can help him up. But pity the man who falls and has no one to help him up! Also, if two lie down together, they will keep warm. But how can one keep warm alone?"

Some of you may think that the above passage has no sexual connotation. But remember that everything in the Bible should be taken in context and must relate to another part. It sounds like Solomon was expressing the attitudes of his father David who had been deeply in love with another man.

I don't know for sure if Jonathan and David had sexual relations because I wasn't there, but the indications are that they did and they liked it. Since God and Jesus do not care if we are gay or straight, I have to think that it didn't matter to God if David and Jonathan were lovers. It was their love and loyalty that mattered to God, and not whether it was consummated sexually.

The Bible is an empty closet. Properly translated, it does not have anything negative to say about homosexuality, but it has many good things to say about people who deeply love each other, even when they are of the same gender. Jesus didn't have anything to say to homosexuals when He was here on Earth either! Jesus never said one word, not one sentence, about homosexuality, even in the red letter editions of the Bible.

Elijah and Elisha

Homosexual contact may have played a role in a miraculous healing performed by another revered Jewish prophet, Elijah (a.k.a. Elias).

1 Kings 17:7-24 tells how a widow's son had become ill. The Bible is not clear on his age. It states that Elijah healed him by taking him to a private chamber, putting him on the bed, stretching himself over him three times, and crying out to God with a request for healing.

In the original Hebrew, *1 Kings 17:19-21* translates as follows. Numbers indicate references in Strong's Concordance:

[Elijah] lay with him sexually (#7901) on his own bed (#4296), and called (#7121) to Jehovah (#3068) [to ask for a healing]…. [Elijah] stretched himself (#4058) on the young man (#3206) three (#7969) times (#6471) and called (#7121) to Jehovah (#3068) [to ask again that the young man be healed]….He then recovered.

This passage expresses the idea that sexual contact between a man and a male youth might have been fine with God because at age 12 a male in Jewish culture came into manhood with his bar-mitzvah.

Elijah is an important Biblical figure who also seems to be gay. Elijah lived a footloose lifestyle with no apparent spouse or children. His primary companion was Elisha, an unmarried male who had lived with his parents until he became Elijah's companion and servant. (*1 Kings 19*) Elisha deeply loved Elijah and refused to leave his side. (*2 Kings 2:1-7*) Doesn't that sound like two gay men to you? It sounds like gay love (homo-affection) to me.

After Elijah ascended to Heaven in a chariot of fire, Elisha also became a Jewish prophet. Elisha traveled with his own personal male companion and servant named Gehazi. In a similar manner to Elijah, Elisha healed a dead youth. *2 Kings 4:32-36* tells us that Elisha and Gehazi entered the young man's room, closed the door, and prayed. Elisha then stretched himself on the boy "mouth to mouth, eyes to eyes, hands to hands." (*2 Kings 4:34, NIV*). Some people think this was an instance of mouth-to-mouth resuscitation, and it might have been. But Elisha's general way of life was definitely something we would think of as being "homosexual" today.

Daniel and Ashpenaz

When Babylon invaded Judah in ancient times, a young man named Daniel was captured with three friends (Shadrack, Meshack and Abednego). They were taken to the palace of Babylonian king Nebuchadnezzar to be educated. Daniel did not want to eat the palace cuisine because it was not prepared according to Jewish law, so he went to one of the court officials, Ashpenaz, who was "master of the eunuchs." (*Daniel 1:8, DRB*).

As the story goes—and I love this story, by the way—the eunuch excused Daniel from eating non-kosher food because the two men had developed a strong bond: "God allowed Daniel to receive faithful love and sympathy from the chief eunuch." (*Daniel 1:9, NJB*). I would call this God looking out for Daniel's welfare. The original Hebrew word translated as "sympathy" is *racham* (Strong's #7356) which comes from *râcham* (Strong's #7355) which means "to fondle." The word suggests that Daniel and the chief eunuch enjoyed sexual intimacy. I like that translation. How lucky can you be? The passage is best translated, "God allowed Daniel to receive faithful love and sexual affection from the chief eunuch." The King James Version says,

"Now God had brought Daniel into favor and tender love with the prince of the eunuchs."

The Bible does not say that Daniel ever had a wife or female lover during his entire life. It appears that Daniel was homosexual. Yay! The smartest, strongest and handsomest men were hand-picked to work in the palace. (*Daniel 1:3-4*). Really? That is what the scripture says.

Since Ashpenaz was a eunuch, you might question whether he and Daniel could have sexually consummated their relationship. Ashpenaz was physically intimate with Daniel, which tells us he was attracted to men. Just because you are castrated after puberty or have had a vasectomy, it does not mean that you have lost your sex drive. Daniel was a handsome young man, and he would have been attractive to many gay men, castrated or not.

Who, exactly, were the Old Testament eunuchs? First of all, most of them were positive characters who found favor with God. In *Isaiah 56,* God blesses eunuchs. Historically, eunuchs were allowed to be passive partners for males. *Isaiah 56:3-8* includes eunuchs in God's covenant, and Jesus allows eunuchs to exist as *an alternative* to a marriage between a man and a woman.

Both the Old and New Testaments speak of "eunuchs." "Eunuch" today refers only to a man who has been castrated. The original Hebrew word for "eunuch" in the Bible was *çâriyç* (Strong's #5631) which comes from a root word meaning "to castrate." But some people believe that Biblical eunuchs might have included non-procreators who had *not* been "snipped." This would include the homosexuals. Why would this be true?

I believe that the prophecy of *Isaiah 56:1-5* is about a future still to come. It says that "eunuchs" will be leaders in God's unified church and their names will be written on the walls in Heaven:

> "For thus saith the LORD unto the eunuchs that keep my Sabbaths, and choose the things that please Me, and take hold of My covenant; Even unto them will I give in mine house [Heaven] and within my walls a place and a name better than of sons and of daughters

[heterosexuals]. I will give them an everlasting name that shall not be cut off. Also the sons of the stranger, that join themselves to the LORD, to serve Him, and to love the name of the LORD, to be his servants, every one that keepeth the Sabbath from polluting it, and taketh hold of my covenant; Even them will I bring to my holy mountain, and make them joyful in my house of prayer: their burnt offerings and their sacrifices shall be accepted upon mine altar; for mine house shall be called a house of prayer for all people. The Lord GOD which gathers the outcasts of Israel saith, yet will I gather others to him, beside those that are gathered unto him." *(Isaiah 56:3-8)*

But in another part of the Old Testament, it says that people who are physically blemished or disabled may not be high priests in the Temple. This would mean that the Bible is talking about whole and fully functioning homosexual people when it talks about the "eunuchs" in Old Testament prophecy. So the "eunuchs" in *Isaiah* cannot mean castrated men. This gives extra meaning to God's words:

"To them I will give within my temple and its walls a memorial and a name that is better than the sons and daughters. I will give them [the homosexuals that are faithful to God] an everlasting name that will not be cut off." *(Isaiah 56:5)*

Look again at the information that the Book of Daniel gives to the homosexual Christian for today. God loves and accepts you exactly as you are. Imagine that! This is good information for everyone!

The Apostle Paul

I have always wondered if the apostle Paul was a closeted gay man. Did you ever consider it possible that the man whose writings are such a large piece of the New Testament could have ever had this sort of "drawback"? We have no real way of knowing, but let's look at all the clues.

Paul wrote, "To keep me from becoming conceited because of these surpassingly great revelations, there was given me a thorn in my flesh, a messenger of Satan, to torment me." (*2 Corinthians* 12:7 NIV)

There has been speculation for centuries as to what Paul really meant by his expression "a thorn in the flesh." Some argue that "flesh" here means the lower nature—so the thorn in the flesh represents carnality—sexual lust perhaps. Paul seems to make this explicit when he writes, "sin produced within me all kinds of lustful desires…" *(Romans 7:8, NRSV).* That's about as explicit as you can get. To my thinking, and in light of other Pauline Epistle scriptures, it is apparent to me that he was dealing with intense sexual issues.

Several verses later, he seems to admit that he occasionally yielded to his feelings: "For I know that nothing good dwells within me, that is, in my flesh. I can will what is right, but I cannot do it." *(Romans 7:18, NRSV).* So I speculate that he was more than likely having a love affair with someone.

The writings of Paul show strong feelings for other males. When he wrote to Philemon about his slave Onesimus, Paul said that Onesimus "is my very heart." (*Philemon 12, NIV*). In *2 Timothy*, he declared deep feelings for Timothy who traveled extensively with Paul. When they were not together, Paul missed him terribly:

"I remember you constantly in my prayers, night and day. I yearn to see you again, recalling your tears, so that I may be filled with joy." *(2 Timothy 1:3-4 NAB)*

Because of his deep affection for Timothy, when Paul neared the end of his life, he sent for Timothy. There is no indication that he also sent for a wife, a woman, or any family member. It was as though Timothy fulfilled all of those needs for Paul. Relationships between people do not have to have physical or sexual expression to be powerful.

But then we also have to wonder about Paul's admitted sexual "lapses."

Orthodox Jewish society in his day was very homophobic because the Old Testament (Jewish) scriptures were already being misinterpreted. A gay Jewish man or woman according to tradition would have had no alternative but to hide any homosexual feelings or expressions, or they might have been stoned to death. It sounds like Paul may have experienced "being in the closet" like so many homosexual people today! If Paul was a homosexual, he would certainly have felt tremendous inward torment, much like gay Christians in our current society.

Many men and women have been brought up in conservative churches and hometowns, and later find themselves in sexually permissive environments like San Francisco, Palm Springs, or New York. In my own case, I was raised in a small conservative town in Montana and later found myself in a very sexually permissive location in California. It was exciting to me at first, but also very disconcerting and uncomfortable. It was a huge change.

Paul probably experienced something like this when he moved out of the strict Jewish society of his youth and into the wider and more permissive world of the Roman Empire.

What's more, if Paul did struggle with being a homosexual, he would certainly not have been able to confess it openly, or his ministry would have been fatally compromised. This sounds a lot like how things are with some of our own Christian preachers today! There are many persons behind the pulpit who struggle with this same issue. If anything is ever said about them in this regard, or if their homosexual behavior is revealed, their lives in ministry are completely destroyed. Just think back on some newspaper headlines we've seen! Believe me when I say that their *whole lives* are destroyed. I can tell you this from so many personal friends' experiences. The only way Paul could have possibly referred to such a private struggle would have been through vague and unclear metaphors like *a thorn in the flesh*.

We all have areas in our lives that are a source of physical pain, emotional discouragement, or moral struggle. We all have our *thorns in the flesh*. By referring to his own source of frustration in such roundabout terms, Paul enables all of us to identify with him—and none more so than the Christian gays. We are so often made to feel evil and forced to struggle with this issue in silence because of the ignorance of others.

Before his conversion on the road to Damascus, Paul was a member of the Sanhedrin (*Acts* 22-24) which was the supreme Jewish judicial, ecclesiastical, and administrative council in ancient Jerusalem. One requirement to be in the Sanhedrin was to be married. But how could Paul have met this requirement when it seems from his writings that he was single? How had he become a part of the Sanhedrin? Perhaps he had been married and his wife had died. Perhaps when he became a Christian she left him. We don't know for certain because Scripture is again silent because your sexual identity is not important to God. So, we don't know if Paul was gay, and it is speculation to say that he was. God, however, chose to bless him, and he writes a majority of the New Testament. You go, Paul!

Jesus and John

If you think this book has been controversial up to this point, hold on to your boots! Now you're really going to be challenged in your thinking! I'm going to suggest some controversial things for your thinking, if I haven't already.

Many Christians will have trouble with the idea that Jesus and John *might* have been lovers. Let me begin by saying that it is possible for two men or two women to have a loving friendship (phillia) without sexual attraction. Just like you and I have a fondness for certain people more than others, it is certainly possible that this was the situation between Jesus and John. It is important to emphasize here that homosexuality is not just a sexual act. It is who we are at the core of our being. A profound intimacy is possible without being sexualized. Does that ease your mind?

The scripture says that Jesus was tempted in every way that is common to man. Men commonly know the importance of sex! I stated earlier that men tend to be led around by their little head and not usually their big head.

Jesus undoubtedly had a very special attachment to John who is referred to in Scripture as *the disciple that Jesus loved.* Jesus is constantly telling people how much he loved

John. Jesus knew that John would become the Apostle of Love. Jesus also saw John as the one who would record the events of the Book of Revelation about the End Times.

Scripture further makes it very clear that there was a special emotional relationship between Jesus and the disciple whom He loved. At the Last Supper, John sat directly next to Jesus and put his head on Jesus' chest. In that culture and at that time, it may have been a common gesture of non-sexual friendship. However, if you saw someone doing that today, you would guess it was a homosexual relationship.

Jesus was comfortable with being kissed by other men. Judas kissing Jesus in the garden at the betrayal showed that this was a common practice. Maybe customs were different in those days, but my point is that those behaviors would be considered "gay" in many countries today.

Without trying to stir up a lot of controversy, we also have to take note of the young man Lazarus. In *John 11:3*, the sisters of Lazarus send word to Jesus, "Lord, the one You love is sick." The *one* You love? That is a term we would use today for someone's spouse or lover. (And that's why some people think that Lazarus was the "disciple" that Jesus loved, not John, but that's a speculation for another time and place.)

What about the unidentified young man in the garden when Jesus was arrested?

"A young man, wearing nothing but a linen garment, was following Jesus. When they seized him, he fled *naked*, leaving his garment behind." *(Mark 14:51-52, NIV)*

Who was he? What was he doing there? Why was he scantily clad? Was it a community park raid? The Bible does not explain. Some people think the young man was Mark because the incident is only recorded in the Gospel of Mark. Or could it have been John? Some people think it was Lazarus. So it's all up for debate since I wasn't there and we don't have all the information surrounding the story. Again the Bible leaves the story with many unanswered questions! But it is a really interesting mystery! By the way, I was in a movie mystery once. *Corky's Hot Ice!* I loved doing that!

We know very little about Jesus during His time from age 12 to age 30 or so when he began His ministry. It was during those years that Jesus would have hit puberty and had to deal with his sexual feelings. It says in *Hebrews 4:1* that Jesus was tempted in every way that is known to man, yet Jesus remained sinless in the flesh. How could both things be true?

Let me remind you that *sex is not a sin!* You can have sex and still be sinless in the flesh as long as the sex meets God's standards! If Jesus had had sex without commitment, he would have been violating those standards. Jesus was *extremely* committed to His followers. He went to the cross for the people around him just as much as Christians believe that Jesus gave His life for us today!

All the clues in the Bible and Apocrypha about Jesus being sexual are speculation. You may want to search this out for yourself. In my experience, much of the Christian world has been hesitant to even talk about sex, much less about Jesus's sexual life. Many people believe that Jesus was pure in the sense of not engaging in sex. Others think that He was married with children. Some think He was gay. There are all kinds of ideas in society. While bailing hay with my father one summer I can remember the hired hands saying something to the effect: You can't tell me that those cowboys on those cattle drives didn't fool around with each other sometimes. They tried to relate this to Jesus and His disciples too. Just keep in mind that we do not know everything there is to know about His life. *John 21:25* says:

> "Jesus did many other things as well. If every one of them were written down, I suppose that even the whole world would not have room for the books that would be written."

To me, it's rather miraculous that the Gospels, having being written by different men at different times, came out in such a way that almost any person can find a reflection of their God-given selves in Jesus. In other words, Jesus becomes truly universal. There is truth about Him! Truth about what He looked like, whether He was married, whether He had a relationship with the Beloved Disciple, etc. But the way the Gospels were inspired, heterosexuals can find a straight man in Jesus. Gays can find a gay man. People who value chastity can find a chaste man. Some people can find a black man. Others can find a man with white skin and red hair. Others can find a man who looked like most people of that region at the time. I think that Christians tend to see these differences as a problem, and they can get very upset if the man they see in the Gospels is not the same man that another person might see. I have never understood why Christians have not embraced the diversity of images that people can find in the Gospels about Jesus. To me, that diversity sends a very important message. It tells you that it actually doesn't matter what Jesus looked like, or what his romantic life was or wasn't. And because it doesn't matter about Him, it doesn't matter about you, either. The Gospels seems to be saying that Jesus could have been any of those things, He could have been the same thing as you; (straight, gay, black, Caucasian, etc.), so the only thing that's important is the Spiritual message. I get so puzzled by Christians sometimes when they are handed such a universal Savior and then they get all pissy about it. Jeesh!

But, the Scriptures *do* tell us everything we need to know for our salvation. It just does not tell us all the personal details about the lives of the prophets.

Jesus never says anything about sexual orientation or homosexuality, and if that had been important to Him or to our salvation, He would have said something! So if Jesus didn't care, why should *we* care? Do you know what it was that Jesus really got angry about? *Hypocrisy!* Some of our "Christian" friends need to take note of this.

There is an interesting story in Scripture where Jesus may have shown that He supported loyal homosexual relationships. Because homosexuality is not specifically mentioned in this story one way or the other, we have to turn to history and tradition to get the true meaning:

> "When Jesus had entered Capernaum, a centurion came to him, asking for help. "Lord," he said, "my servant lies at home paralyzed and in terrible suffering." Jesus said to him, "I will go and heal him." The centurion replied, "Lord, I do not deserve to have you come under my roof. But just say the word, and my servant

will be healed. For I myself am a man under authority, with soldiers under me. I tell this one, 'Go,' and he
goes; and that one, 'Come,' and he comes. I say to my
servant, 'Do this,' and he does it." When Jesus heard
this, He was astonished and said to those following
him, "I tell you the truth, I have not found anyone in
Israel with such great faith." Jesus said, "You have great
faith. Go home. I've healed him." *(Matthew 8:5-10)*

There are some hints in the Greek words for "my servant" to show that the servant had more of a relationship
with the centurion than just master-servant. In Luke's Gospel,
the centurion's slave "is dear" *(Luke 7:1-10 RSV)* to the centurion. I believe this could very well have been the centurion's
lover, and Jesus healed him on the spot knowing that the
centurion would continue to have sexual relations with the
slave. It is a historical fact that centurions had lovers—other
men who traveled with them just for the purpose of love
making and relieving stress between battles. Yet Jesus did
not express any prohibitions on the relationship.

Don't ever think that Jesus was living in an isolated bub-
ble! He lived in a diverse culture, in a seaport town, where
the Greeks and Romans had planted their cultures. Homosexual relationships were commonplace. Greek art and literature reveal that male-to-male sexual relationships were
accepted as a customary practice. The Greeks and Romans
had a word in their language for male-to-male loving sexual
relationships. That word is *not* our term for "homosexuality"
as it is used or understood today. Psychologists view homosexuality as an orientation of personality rather than an act,
mental illness, or sickness.

Jesus could have commented on homosexuality at any time as He walked through the crowds of people because people were there with their lovers. Jesus didn't think it was important enough to even bother commenting about! Again, if Jesus didn't think it was important, why do we? Labeling people and putting them into a box was not Jesus' intent. People are people. We all are in need of a Savior and Jesus knew that!

Should we be shocked that some of the people in the Bible might have been gay—that they might have been different from the majority of people that way? Consider this:

How many people do you know that are left-handed? We understand that the great majority of people in the world are right-handed and that left-handedness is just a variation. It's not wrong to be left-handed. It's not a defect to be left-handed. It is simply one of God's *many variations* in creation. It is just different. Left-handed people use a different portion of their brains to accomplish different tasks. Yet at one time, the Christian church believed that left-handedness was of the devil. People who were left-handed went through all sorts of torture just to conform to the thinking of that day. This type of thinking is ridiculous, absurd, and silly to us today. I am so grateful for today's generation where people are more educated and enlightened in these matters.

As a child growing up in Montana, one of the things we would do when it snowed was run around and collect snowflakes. It brings a smile to me now because they would always melt before we could show them off to our playmates or parents. Scientists have shown us that if you are able to preserve snowflakes, you would never find two that are exactly the same. If you could see all the snowflakes that have ever fallen, *never* have there been two snowflakes that were identical. All I know is that I had to shovel the snow from the sidewalk.

In grade school, our teacher would have us do art projects by cutting out snowflakes on construction paper and placing them around the class room. None of them were exactly the same.

All of this confirms to me that *God delights in variety.* God is a God of diversity. We would get bored if everything and everyone were identical. God never intended to create a cookie-cutter world filled with cookie-cutter people. Scripture says that we are His workmanship, created for His pleasure!

> "For we are His workmanship, created in Christ Jesus unto good works, which God hath before ordained that we should walk in them." (*Ephesians 2:10*)

Jesus said that in the days before His return, knowledge would increase. And I think that this is happening now. Computers and the internet are creating an information explosion. All of this expanding knowledge is circulating at a faster pace all around the globe just as Jesus predicted. The same kind of research that has changed the faulty teachings on subjects like left-handedness will change the faulty teachings that now condemns homosexuality.

So I state again that you, gay or straight, have value to your lives just like all the people of God. You have something to offer that no one else does. You are someone's special somebody! You were made in the image of God, and God approved of you! You didn't just happen to be a glimmer in your parents' eyes. God had already been thinking about you before you were ever born.

Psalms 139:16-17 states that God had ordained all of our days even before the beginning of the Earth. You were put together on purpose! You are an original. You are one of a kind. There is no one else like you. If you are straight or a homosexual, it's because God created you to be that way! A Homosexual!

The same is true if you are a heterosexual. It's not a choice! You need to take the bull by the horns and stop thinking all those negative and critical things about yourself. Start looking at yourself as a one-of-a-kind creation of God. Sure, you may not be perfect, but neither am I. I just don't tell anyone. We are all sinners. No, it isn't because we were born with the guilt of Adam's sin. It's because we have all sinned and have come short of the glory of God. (*Romans 3:23*)

I read a little thing the other day about a man who scribbled a note to his preacher after a sermon. The note read, "I hope you're happy! After your sermon on 'A half-truth is a whole lie,' I had to put my true weight on my driver's license." I laughed at the story.

I know I have areas in my life where I need to improve. But I enjoy being me. The Bible tells me that since I belong to Christ, I am accepted and approved just as God created me. So no matter how many mistakes you make, you have God's DNA. You are a joint heir with Jesus Christ! Don't you just want to shout?!

Chapter 10
The Apostle Paul on Homosexuality
Part 1: Romans

❧❧

In the previous chapter, we discussed the possibility that Paul may have been a latent or closeted homosexual who struggled with his sexuality: "...sin produced within me all kinds of lustful desire..." (*Romans 7:8, NRSV*). Paul comes across like many of our television evangelists today who speak out on a certain topics that are personal for them—topics that they are struggling with internally. Paul clearly had anti-sex issues, and I believe they arose because of his unresolved homosexual feelings, much like many people today. Even if Paul seemed to speak out against homosexuality in his letters, that doesn't disprove that he had those feelings himself. How many religious and political leaders with a Christian following in recent times have spoken out against homosexuality only to be caught later in a paid affair with a 15-year-old boy, or sending suggestive emails to male pages, or "toe-tapping" in an airport bathroom, or hiring a young man from Rentaboy.com? These things sound funny, and on the surface they are when the late night comedians tell jokes on national television. Most people who talk so deliberately about a particular subject are usually the ones who are dealing with these subjects themselves personally. My heart still goes out to these people who are obviously struggling with their own sexuality!

Paul may have been struggling with his sexuality, but his public statements may not be as anti-gay as some people have made them out to be. In fact, they may not be anti-gay at all! Here are some statements from Paul that some people quote when they talk about homosexuality.

"For although they knew God, they neither glorified Him as God nor gave thanks to Him, but their thinking became futile and their foolish hearts were darkened, Although they claimed to be wise, they became fools and exchanged the glory of the immortal God for images made to look like mortal man and birds and animals and reptiles. Therefore God gave them over in the sinful desires of their hearts to sexual impurity for the degrading of their bodies with one another. They exchanged the truth of God for a lie and worshiped and served created things rather than the Creator, who is forever praised. Amen.

Because of this, God gave them over to shameful lusts. Even their women exchanged natural relations for unnatural ones. In the same way the men also abandoned natural relations with women and were inflamed with lust for one another. Men committed indecent acts with other men, and received in themselves the due penalty for their perversion. Furthermore, since they did not think it worthwhile to retain the knowledge of God, He gave them over to a depraved mind to do what ought not to be done. They have become filled

with every kind of wickedness, evil, greed and depravity. They are full of envy, murder, strife, deceit and malice. They are gossips, slanderers, God-haters, insolent, arrogant and boastful; they invent ways of doing evil; they disobey their parents; they are senseless, faithless, heartless, and ruthless. Although they know God's righteous decree that those who do such things deserve death, they not only continue to do those very things but also approve of those who practice them."
Romans 1:21-32 (NIV).

Well-meaning people who condemn homosexuality have been pulling this scripture completely out of context for centuries. Can you say *context*? They seem to know little or nothing about the context in which this passage was written. Did I happen to mention the word *context*?

Paul is still talking about idolatry! He says, "…they became fools and exchanged the glory of the immortal God for images made to look like mortal man and birds and animals and reptiles. *Therefore…*"

So let me walk you through this!

It's the word "therefore" in verse 24 that's important. The people had strayed far from God; *therefore* those people set up other gods as idols and began to act in ways that were *unnatural for them as part of that false worship.* Paul is just saying that you must not practice idolatry; otherwise you will find yourself becoming a person that you are not meant to be!

Most people in Paul's audience were heterosexuals. He used examples of heterosexuals practicing homosexuality. This is *exactly* what was happening in the cultic temples. Most people who indulged in those activities didn't have a homosexual orientation! Those pagan sexual acts were therefore *"unnatural"* to all of the heterosexuals. The heterosexual person exchanged what was *natural* for them to what was *unnatural* for them.

Please don't mistake or misunderstand this. That's where people today get all perplexed and mixed up! They have been given incorrect information and get confused, because who we are and what we do are two different things.

Heterosexual people cannot change their sexual orientation just by having sex with a person of the same sex! Also, homosexual people cannot change their sexual orientation just by having sex with a person of the opposite sex! Sexual orientation is inborn. This is true even if you are gay and trying to "pray the gay away." The same is true if you are straight and believe that having engaged in sexual activities with a person of the same gender makes you gay. We see this in prisons all the time where homosexual behavior is commonplace due to the circumstances of incarceration, but most of the people participating in that behavior (homosexuality) are still straight *and remain straight*! This is sexual activity by convenience, not orientation!

Conservatives may want to believe that sexual orientation is controlled by choice. Sorry, sexual orientation cannot be changed either by an act of will or fear of consequences. Gay people could possibly force themselves to engage in different behaviors, but it would not be *natural* to them and might even feel shameful or repulsive to them. What you need to know is that a truly gay person feels just as instinctively disgusted at the thought of having heterosexual sex as a straight person does about having homosexual sex. Believe me I know!

That is what Paul was talking about in *Romans* Chapter One! It is natural for each of us to be comfortable with sexual activity according to our God-given orientation. I can tell you that from experience. On my journey I was encouraged by a couple of counselors to try heterosexual sex. I did, only to feel guilt and shame.

We don't choose to be gay any more than a heterosexual person chooses to be straight. That's why the message of "ex-gay" groups in reparative therapy is so harmful. If people had the power to choose their orientation, almost every gay person would choose to be straight.

Heterosexuality is held up as the preferred behavior despite all its many faults. In some Christian communities, you are somehow flawed and broken if you do not embrace the sexual norm. This would be fine for those among us who have not been gifted with a homosexual orientation!

I am often reminded of that children's song in the 70's that states God does not make mistakes. God is not an Indian giver. God has blessed us and created us to be who we are. Our sexual orientation is just one of our many blessings of who we are. We are born the way we are born and we can love who we choose to love.

The people that Paul describes had gone so far from God that the confusion in their mind was *reflected* by their behavior. These people had gone so far away from God that they were looking for any stimulating experience that might fill the emptiness in their hearts. This is much like other things that people abuse in our society today, one of them being drugs. I have said it already, but again let me state, "There is a God shaped vacuum in the heart of every human being that only God can fill."

Some of our more paranoid "Christian" brothers and sisters think that the gay population wants to "recruit" heterosexuals into becoming homosexuals. What a bunch of gibberish and nonsense! It is just as impossible to make someone gay as it is to make someone ex-gay! We only preach that people should act according to their true God-given natures. Heterosexuals should always behave like heterosexuals, and homosexuals should always behave like homosexuals, according to every person's unique personality. That is the real message of Paul.

Let me point out who are the *real* recruiters. It's the Right-Wing Christians who run the ex-gay ministries! They are trying to recruit and persuade everyone into being heterosexuals! They want everyone to engage in heterosexual behavior regardless of orientation.

Returning to *Romans 1,* many theologians have instructed us to remember that every time you come to the word "they" or "them," you can substitute the word "pagan" or "pagans," as we will do here for *Romans* 1:18-28:

"The wrath of God is being revealed from heaven against all the godlessness and wickedness of men who suppress the truth by pagan wickedness, since what may be known about God is plain to [pagans], because God has made it plain to [pagans]. For since the creation of the world God's invisible qualities—His eternal power and divine nature—have been clearly seen, being understood from what has been made, so that men are without excuse. Although they, the [pagans], knew God, they neither glorified Him as God nor gave thanks to Him, but their thinking became futile and their foolish hearts were darkened. Although they claimed to be wise, the [pagans] became fools and exchanged the glory of the immortal God for images made to look like mortal man and birds and animals and reptiles. Therefore God gave the [pagans] over in the sinful desires of their hearts to sexual impurity for the degrading of their bodies with one another. The [pagans] exchanged the truth of God for a lie, and worshiped and served created things rather than the Creator—who is forever praised. Amen."

The people being referred to in *Romans 1:26* are *not* homosexuals. This passage refers almost entirely to heterosexuals, not to gays. Those people were not expressively, spiritually, emotionally, mentally, or physically inclined toward their own sex, since they are depicted as having abandoned their *natural* practices. So I ask myself this question: why has the Religious Right not seen this? They fail to see context!

The Pauline epistles do not explicitly treat the question of homosexual activity between two persons of the same sex who share a homosexual orientation. Same-gender sex between two individuals with the same sexual orientation is not "abandoning" their natural custom, so you cannot legitimately read this section as condemning homosexuality *per se.*

This section of scripture once again goes back to idolatry. When women became priestesses or temple prostitutes and had ritual sex, it was the act of turning away from natural loving sex to unnatural temple sex. Even though it was *straight* sex, it was still wrong in God's eyes.

The same is true of cultic male prostitutes. Their sexual activity became unnatural because it involved idolatry. When heterosexual men went to the pagan temples several times a day for sexual worship with male prostitutes, it was *unnatural* for them and was idolatry. This is the kind of thing Paul was addressing in *Romans.*

I know this is a lot of information, but I hope you are still with me!

Romans 1:26 repeats an important point. It says, "Because of this, God gave them over to shameful lusts." You just have to step back to see what "because of this" is actually referring to. When we do, we discover that it has the same effect as the word "therefore" in verse 24. It's all connected to idolatry and pagan worship!

OK, now we'll step back again, this time to verse 21 and look at "although." Oh, look. Paul is *still* talking about paganism!

We're not done yet. Now we'll step back even further to verse 18, and you know what, we get the same result *again!* Are you following me? It means that all of this scripture in *Romans* follows one continuous thought, and that thought is about paganism and idol worship. As we can see, the entire passage in *Romans 1* is not talking about true homosexuality whatsoever.

Some people think that homosexuality is unnatural because it can involve sodomy. "Sodomy" is a term used in the secular law to describe an act of "unnatural" sex. It can be oral sex, anal sex, or any non-genital to genital contact, whether heterosexual or homosexual.

When I talk about sodomy below, I mean anal intercourse. I have had my straight "Christian" friends mention to me that it's not *natural* for a man to put his genital organ into a place where another person excretes. They say God didn't create the human body for that kind of activity.

They would argue, "That alone should let you know, from a physical standpoint, that homosexuals are perverted and ungodly. A man needs to be with a woman for 'natural' sex!" Rubbish!

First of all, most lesbians that I have talked to stimulate the genitals during sex. There is no anal contact involved. The argument about anal intercourse doesn't apply to those couples. Sex between most gay men is also intended to stimulate the partners' genitals. Genitals are the pleasure centers in nearly all gay sex just like they are in straight sex.

Let's also make it clear that sodomy is practiced within both the straight and gay worlds. I am amazed by the ignorance in this area. In the straight world, there is a whole industry that makes heterosexual porn showing men having anal intercourse with women. So "sodomite" does not equal "gay." Please get that straight! (Pun intended.)

Not all gay male couples engage in sodomy. Probably more of them do than straight couples, but it is not 100%. Many gay men also have issues with cleanliness. There are many other ways that they can and do achieve great sexual pleasure with each other partner.

Medical and physical science has shown us that no human cavity is intrinsically clean. Looking back at *Leviticus,* when a woman was in one portion of her monthly cycle, she was believed to be unclean. A man was unclean if he was uncircumcised. If the foreskin of a man was not removed, then he was considered unclean. If a man had an emission or an ejaculation during the night while he was dreaming, he was considered unclean as well. I have had several of those. All these attitudes tended to encourage sexual reproduction amongst the Israelites because sexual intercourse happened when the woman was fertile. Also, the Israelites were in the desert and had to conserve water. Circumcision helped with sanitation and remaining healthy.

Today, the whole subject of hygiene is viewed differently. We have condoms not only to stop the spread of disease, but also for cleanliness to the genital organs and to prevent pregnancy. When the Bible was written, the idea of a condom was not even a consideration.

So what about people, gay and straight, who *do* engage in sodomy? Many people solve the dilemma of cleanliness by cleaning inside the anal canal area before sex, or by using a condom. It is a fact that stimulation of the prostate from anal penetration is pleasurable to many people, and so the act becomes pleasurable for both parties. So, we can't say that it is *unnatural*. It "fits" and can give pleasure to both parties, just like heterosexual vaginal sex. It is almost as though God designed everything so that all options are possible, including the option for gay men to enjoy the same kind of intimacy and pleasure that vaginal sex offers to straight couples.

Let me say once again, God doesn't look at sex as a sin. God created sex not only for procreation, but also for pleasure. That's why God made it feel good! God wants us to enjoy sexual pleasures. God is only concerned when these gifts are abused.

You can and should share your bodies with your partner for the purpose of mutual joy and satisfaction. It is your mutual experimentation that determines what you find exciting or interesting. It is hard for me to believe that some people don't like sex. With some couples, it's not important, for others, their whole world revolves around an active sex life. Aren't people interesting?

'Nuff said.

Let me balance this out with what the four Gospels say. *Matthew, Mark, Luke* and *John* are the books in which the stories and sayings of Jesus are located. They make no explicit statements about homosexuality.

It was decades after Jesus' resurrection that the book of *Romans* was written by Paul to the believers in the city of Rome who had formed the local church. Rome in that day could easily have been considered one of the most corrupt cities and societies that had ever existed. Historic tradition will tell you all you want to know about the practices of the Romans.

Romans one give us a glimpse of the worship that took place in the pagan temples of Rome. Some of it included ceremonial sexual activity. There were many male and female prostitutes who serviced the temple worshippers when they came to bow down before their many idols and false gods. Like in the day of the Old Testament, there was a pagan god of fertility from whom the Romans sought fruitfulness in their farms, families, fields and their livestock.

There is also a context issue at stake in some of the things that Paul wrote, just like there was with *Leviticus.* Paul said that it was natural for a woman to have long hair. Because of this, some Christian women today will not cut their hair short. In contrast, there are many other women who do cut their hair and do have short hair. It is just a matter of style. How judgmental would we be to call women "evil" who prefer shorter hair?

What about your mothers? Did she have short hair, particularly in her elderly years?

Likewise, many men have long hair, and that is also considered acceptable. Look at the many pictures of Jesus with his long flowing hair! Cultural customs down through time have changed. For the most part, hair length is not important. What Paul considered long hair was shoulder length or greater. In more recent times, men have had what we now consider short hair; however, I suspect that Paul never saw a crew cut!

So, is homosexuality *ever* wrong?

The answer is: homosexuality is wrong whenever heterosexuality is wrong. The standards that are set for the heterosexual are the same standards set for the homosexual. What's good for the goose is good for the gander! Taking any Biblical verse out of context to make it stand alone is unconscionable and unacceptable.

When my "Christian" friends say that God hates the homosexuals, they are declaring something inconsistent with God's very nature. God cannot behave in a hateful way if God is love. The Bible specifically says that God *is* love. Then God cannot hate homosexuals! *(John 4:14)* Don't ever forget that! So why, then, do so many "Christians" hate homosexuals who God created in His image? *(Genesis 1:27)* Isn't this just as mind-boggling? Those Christians are not honoring or embracing the message of the very scriptures that they claim to believe as gospel!

Let me remind you that, first of all, we are Christians. None of us who call ourselves "Christians" are perfect, but God says we are accepted, approved and loved!

Still not convinced? So you still are bothered by what Paul says in *Romans?* Well, wait until you read what Paul says in *Corinthians!*

Chapter 11
The Apostle Paul on Homosexuality Part 2: Corinthians

❦

The book of Corinthians was one of Paul's letters addressed to the local church in Corinth. Corinth was a major Greek seaport and a crossroad to the Roman Empire.

Corinth was also an idolatrous and sexually immoral city. The major temple in Corinth alone—not counting all the lesser temples—had ten thousand priests and priestesses who were sexual servants to those who came to "worship"…for a fee. Corinth was so bad that even the Romans considered the place evil. If the Romans wanted to say that a woman was of ill repute, they would call her a "Corinthian girl."

In *1 Corinthians 6:9-10,* Paul writes:

"Do you not know that the wicked will not inherit the kingdom of God? Do not be deceived. Neither the sexually immoral nor idolaters nor adulterers nor *male prostitutes* nor *homosexual offenders* nor thieves nor the greedy nor drunkards nor slanderers nor swindlers will inherit the kingdom of God."

Paul writes similar words to Timothy—his youthful apprentice, traveling companion, and possible lover:

> "Now the purpose of the commandment is love from a pure heart, from a good conscience, and from sincere faith, from which some, having strayed, have turned aside to idle talk, desiring to be teachers of the law, understanding neither what they say nor the things which they affirm. But we know that the law is good if one uses it lawfully, knowing this: that the law is not made for a righteous person, but for the lawless and insubordinate, for the ungodly and for sinners, for the unholy and profane, for murderers of fathers and murderers of mothers, for manslayers, for fornicators, for *sodomites*, for kidnappers, for liars, for perjurers, and if there is any other thing that is contrary to sound doctrine, according to the glorious gospel of the blessed God which was committed to my trust." (*1 Timothy 1:5-11 NKJV*)

The above two passages have caused many LGBT people needless pain. This scripture has been quoted as proof texts that homosexuals cannot have a place in Heaven. We must not let incorrect interpretations of these passages, or any other passages for that matter, rob us of our inheritance that is freely given in other portions of the Bible. As we will soon see, these two passages address the same issues as the passages from *Romans* that we looked at in the previous chapter. They are *not* about people in loving same-sex relationships.

In *Galatians 5:19 (RSV)*, Paul lists the sexually immoral situations that existed in Corinth:

"The acts of the sinful nature are obvious: sexual immorality, impurity and debauchery; idolatry and witchcraft; hatred, discord, jealousy fits of rage, selfish ambition, dissension's, factions and envy, drunkenness, orgies and the like. I warn you as I did before that those who live like this will not inherit the kingdom of God."

Paul is describing people who live without moral standards. If you study the Greek meanings to these words, not one of them identifies homosexuality or homophilia. (*Homo,* meaning "man" or "the same," and *philia* meaning "love.") What Paul saw and addressed in this text were *heterosexual* men engaging in *homosexual* acts or involuntary (forced) sexual submission in the context of pagan orgies and idol worship.

In one passage where Paul says that these men had "committed" indecent acts, the word for "committed" in the Greek is *kater-gazomai.* There are two words here: *gazomai* means "it takes a lot of work," and *Kater* means "extreme energy required to accomplish a task." What this tells me is that the heterosexual men had a hard time achieving an erection with other men, and when they managed to do so, they had a hard time keeping that erection and achieving an orgasm. In other words, it is difficult work to engage in sex outside of your natural orientation.

Let's look at the words and expressions used by Paul in the *Corinthians* "clobber passages" to understand what he was really saying.

#1. Sexually Immoral.

The Greek word *pornela* is used in this context. It means taking pleasure in pornographic pictures or writings. This has nothing to do with a committed loving relationship; it has more to do with obsessive/compulsive behavior in regard to pornographic images. Yes, people were making porn even back in those days! This is apparent in the art graphics of the day. This applies to men and women, single and married. It addresses the nature of the heart with its desires and thoughts.

#2. Adulterers.

We probably all know what adultery is. It is when married people violate their covenant of faithfulness and become sexually involved with someone other than their spouse. Adultery also applies to the thoughts and intents of the heart and mind. We are exhorted throughout scripture to guard our hearts and minds, for it is from that area that our behavior will be expressed. *(Philippians 4:6-8)* A thought can eventually become an action.

I wonder how many adulterers might be reading this book. I wonder how many people are sitting in the pews of mainline churches today who are adulterers. I find it curious and hypocritical that the same fundamentalists who condemn the gay Christian with *1 Corinthians 6:9-10* entirely miss the word "adulterer" on that same list. Many straight Christians fit this label, and they are happily accepted as leaders in mainline Christian churches. Their lives and thoughts may or may not be known to the people around them.

There is a double standard within the church. To look at the same scripture and say that the gay person is eternally lost, while the adulterer is welcomed into the church with open arms, is hypocrisy.

#3. Idolaters.

We all know that idolaters are people who worship false idols, images, and gods. Some people believe that it can also include putting material things before God.

#4. Male prostitutes and homosexual offenders.

Certain things that Paul wrote have always been difficult to understand. Even the Apostle Peter, when talking about Paul, thought so:

> "His letters contain some things that are hard to understand, which ignorant and unstable people distort, as they do the other Scriptures, to their own destruction."
> (*2 Peter 3:16 NIV*)

The Religious Right takes the reference to "male prostitutes and homosexual offenders" out of context. They want to condemn homosexuals as a class of people who will not inherit the kingdom of God. But the word "homosexual" was not even used in the translations of these scriptures until 1946 when the Revised Standard Version ("RSV") was published!

So, what did Paul really mean? We can look to *1 Timothy* for clues. Two of the Greek words here are *arsénókóités and malakos.*

The word *arsénókóités* was evidently invented by Paul or Timothy. It doesn't exist anywhere else in Greek literature, and it may have been a code word between the two of them, like a little love talk. I have those sorts of codes and words that I use as love talk with people I am close too. In fact, *arsénókóités* was not used again until about A.D. 383 when Saint

Jerome gave it the meaning "male prostitute." *Arsénókóités* is really a combination of two words: *arsén* (Strong's #730) which means a strong male (capable of "lifting") and *kóité* (Strong's #2845) which comes from the word "couch," but has a connotation of "cohabitation" or even "male sperm." *Arsénókóités* probably means a macho man who "cohabitates" or is the source of sperm. So in *1 Timothy*, Paul is really talking about catamites (*malakós*) (boys kept for sexual pleasure/prostitutes) and the virile males (*arsénókóités*) who lie down or have sex with them. Since improper worship is the focus of this passage, it is repeating the Old Testament sanction against temple prostitution.

The cultic priests and prostitutes were heavily involved in pagan worship and used their sexuality as a hook to draw other people into pagan practices. We all know that sex is a strong draw, even in today's society. By carefully reading the scriptures, we can see that the real issue for Paul was temple prostitution.

We also have the Dead Sea Scrolls to compare to Bible translations. We discover that the Bible translations commonly used today are not always as accurate as some of the older ones, like the King James Version. King James hired scholars to make a translation that the common people could read and understand. Although the title page of *The King James Bible* boasted that it was "Newly translated out of the original tongues," the work was actually a revision of *The Bishops Bible* used in Scotland in 1568, which was a revision of *The Great Bible*, which was used in England in 1539. King James wanted a single bible to unify the country.

It is important to know that the men who produced the King James Bible not only inherited some of the errors made by previous English translators, but I am sure invented some on their own. Now that doesn't mean that the Bible is not inspired. The scripture says in *2 Timothy 3:14-17*:

"But you must remain faithful to the things you have been taught. You know they are true, for you know you can trust those who taught you. You have been taught the holy Scriptures from childhood, and they have given you the wisdom to receive the salvation that comes by trusting in Christ Jesus. All Scripture is inspired by God and is useful to teach us what is true and to make us realize what is wrong in our lives. It corrects us when we are wrong and teaches us to do what is right. God uses it to prepare and equip His people to do every good work."

Despite the fact that the words are not all correct, the principles are still there! So don't throw the baby out with the bath water. As long as the translations are in sync, we will be led by the Spirit. Without King James, the most widely-sold Bible in Christian history would never have been produced. Many people throughout the centuries have come to the saving and loving knowledge of Jesus Christ by means of this Bible. For many years there were no significant competitors to the KJV. The revised version came out much later.

The King James Version ("KJV") translates the word *malakós* in a somewhat different way. We find *malakós* in *Matthew 11:8 KJV* when John the Baptist says, "But what went you out for to see? A man clothed in soft raiment? Behold, they that wear soft clothing are in kings' houses." Even in this version, Paul's writing has nothing to do with homosexuality; it was about the rich and powerful people who wore soft clothing.

Malakós is also found in *1 Corinthians 6* (KJV) where it has been mistranslated as "effeminate" even though it is based on a Greek word that means literally "soft." Since the same Greek word is translated as "soft clothing" in the King James translation of the Gospels, it can mean people who are spoiled or pampered, but it was also sometimes slang for being morally loose. It had nothing to do with sexual orientation even though some Bibles go as far as to mistranslate the word in *1 Corinthians 6:9* as "homosexual"!

So why the discrepancy in how *malakós* is translated? It is exactly the same word, yet translators give it different meanings in different parts of scripture. *Matthew* is referring to clothing, and *1 Corinthians* is referring to persons, but they both connote softness. So what was Paul trying to say? We can only make several guesses:

#1. Perhaps he was talking about people who have no back bone. They don't stand up for what they know is right!

#2. Perhaps he was describing a wishy-washy person. This could be said about a person who knows about God but doesn't want a relationship with God. They show no consistency or commitment.

#3. Some were "jelly-like." With a sword at his throat, Peter also ran away from Jesus Christ and denied Him in the courtyard outside the trial. It was cowardice.

Each of these could be defined as a "soft" person. Paul later wrote to the church at Corinth:

"And that is what some of you were. But you were washed, you were sanctified, you were justified in the name of the Lord Jesus Christ and by the Spirit of our God. Everything is permissible for me—but not every-thing is beneficial. Everything is permissible for me—but I will not be mastered by anything." (*1 Corinthians 6:11*)

Paul is calling for *balance* in our lives. He says that cer-tain people will have trouble getting into Heaven: thieves, the greedy, drunkards, slanderers, gossips, and swindlers. Yet in our day, I don't hear too much being preached to Christians about this. When is your local anti-gay pastor going to say that all *greedy* people are also going to Hell? After all, greed and gossiping are included in Paul's list. But nooooooo, the anti-gay pastor's mind is made up and stuck on "homosexual offender" even though Paul is not referring to homosexual *orientation*.

Some Christians make the assumption that *1 Corinthi-ans 6:9* is saying that only certain people will inherit the kingdom of God. However, the issue that Paul was really ad-dressing was that people should simply respect their own bodies, which had nothing to do with sexual orientation. He wrote in *1 Corinthian 6:19-20*:

"Do you not know that your body is a temple of the Holy Spirit, who is in you, whom you have received from God? You are not your own; you were bought at a price. Therefore honor God with your body."

Paul is contrasting the wickedness of idolatry against the believers.

God never refers to believers as "the wicked." This section of scripture is addressing *non*-believers. Homosexual believers are *not* included here because they have received Jesus Christ as their personal Lord and Savior. This scripture does not refer to them at all!

Paul was a very scholarly man. He had been to school and knew the meaning of words. If Paul had wanted to say "homosexuality," he would have said *homophilia*. The word *homophilia* is not used in the entire Greek New Testament, including in the Gospels when Jesus speaks. Look for yourself!

Then why did so many Bible translators take such liberties? Why did they wrongly translate so many Biblical words into "homosexuality"? Were the translators embarrassed for God? Did they think God had miscommunicated His intent to His people, so they wanted to help Him on these obscure passages? Isn't that just so kind and sweet of the translators? They were *presuming* what God meant in His love letter to us, instead of what God actually inspired his messengers to write and say.

Then why are many "Christian" representatives of Jesus Christ compounding this error by hurting and killing so many people over this today? Take a moment to think about that. When I say "killing," I don't mean direct physical attacks. I am talking about wrong teachings that inspire some people to kill and commit suicide. Today we hear about gay teen suicides caused by bullying and depression. Many homosexual youth have killed themselves because they could not change their sexual orientation no matter how much they prayed or how hard they tried. For many of these kids, the despair was

brought on by the hatred and mean-spiritedness of homophobic ministers, priests, and religious teachers.

In my own youth, having come from a fundamental
church background, I struggled deeply with anti-gay teachings. I fasted and prayed asking God to take away this curse
from me. However, my sexual feelings never changed. Although people said that homosexuality was a sin, I could
not get delivered from it. I kept trying to follow rules that
did not work for me. In my later life I realized that God said I
was OK. I knew I would go to Heaven one day, but I needed
help living in the here and now.

I remember in the early days of my LGBT congregation,
Celebration of Faith, one person made the comment in a
heated Bible study debate, "Well, that's only what Paul said.
Jesus didn't say anything about the subject, so we can just
ignore what Paul said."

Not so! I believe that holy men of God wrote the Bible
as they were inspired by the Holy Spirit to write, according
to what God intended. Holy Spirit, I honor you! The problem
comes from the later translations created by less inspired
men. *2 Peter 1:20* says:

> "Above all, you must understand that no prophecy of
> Scripture came about by the prophet's own interpre-
> tation. For prophecy never had its origin in the will of
> man, but men spoke from God as they were carried
> along by the Holy Spirit."

I believe that the Bible is the inspired Word of God and
can be taken literally as long as it is *translated and interpreted*
correctly. We read in *Hebrews 1:1&2 NIV:*

"In the past God spoke to our ancestors through the prophets at many times and in various ways, but in these last days He has spoken to us by His Son, whom He appointed heir of all things, and through whom also He made the universe."

What Paul says, in my estimation, is just as inspired as what Jesus said. Sure, Paul was not Jesus. *Jesus* is the very son of God and our Savior. Paul was just a normal guy, a human being, more than likely gay and was dealing with it the best way he knew how. But the writings of Paul are just as important as are the red-lettered words of Jesus. Paul and the other prophets were inspired to share the heart of God through the means available to them. God did not dictate word for word what to write down. God "inspired" men, and trusted them to write as best as they could. God has protected that information ever since. It has held the test of time, so God's blessing obviously is on His Word!

I hope you are seeing how extremely dangerous it is to take one word or group of words out of a verse and pin it on someone like a scarlet letter. We all have our own scarlet letters; and we are all on one of Paul's lists somewhere! But, thank God that through the blood of Jesus, any sin is no longer held against us. Through God's grace and forgiveness, we do have our names listed in the Lamb's Book of Life, and there is no verse in scripture that says it can or will be erased!

As I am thinking about God's love for everyone, I am reminded of a wonderful hymn that we sang in at the Assembly of God church in Lewistown where I grew up:

"Grace, grace, God's grace.
Grace that will pardon and cleanse within;
Grace, grace, God's grace,
Grace that is greater than all my/our sin."

Today I know that God's grace is greater than my worst sin. God's grace is even greater than my darkest shame. I know that "I am forgiven." I know because I have experienced His grace personally.

Chapter 12

What About The One Person Act?

Now, you are in for a real reality check. You may be asking yourself, why would someone who calls himself a minister be speaking about masturbation? Well, it's because no one else seems to be addressing this embarrassing topic. Let me tell you, that in my many years of pastoring I have been asked about masturbation as much as I have been asked if a person can be gay and Christian. This chapter will address my personal perspective. You may have your own views or belief. This may seem to be a little bit of a digression from the topic of this book, but it's not by much.

Masturbation! What a word! Ninety percent of the men in the world masturbate, married or unmarried, and the other ten percent are lying.

In my opinion, the Bible doesn't specifically condemn masturbation, nor does the Bible specifically disregard it. This tends to be one of those "taboo" subjects that people do not like to talk about because of the shame or embarrassment. Please forgive me for making you uncomfortable, but I think it needs to be discussed. I feel like we need to get real; to get down to the basics at a level where we actually live.

Personally, I don't believe that God cringes at the subject of masturbation, or any other subject for that matter. God is big enough to understand! God can take it! Please set your embarrassment aside for a moment so that we can investigate God's view on the matter. Possibly you will be surprised at my conclusions, or perhaps you'll disagree with me, but it's important that we don't allow our feelings of embarrassment to dictate our beliefs.

According to what I know of the Roman Catholic traditions, as well as a few other religions, all sexual acts and thoughts are sinful except those undertaken in marriage with the possibility of procreation. I believe that this extreme interpretation of the Bible is incorrect.

I can remember some sort of "medical guideline" many decades ago saying that men should not have intercourse more than twelve times a year! Some doctors even went as far as to recommend certain foods to "curb the urge." Graham crackers and corn flakes were two of the foods on the list. I guess we all know how wealthy the Kellogg's company became! But I don't think it worked. I can tell you from experience that those corn-fed Midwestern boys could still be pretty horny!

While growing up, I had always assumed that masturbation was a sin. Some of my friends from the Catholic Church and other fundamentalist churches would tell me that *"spilling your seed on the ground"* is a sin. But the truth is, the Bible never explicitly states if masturbation is or is not a sin.

Masturbation is mentioned in *Genesis 38:9-10* in the story of Onan. Onan refused to impregnate his deceased brother's surviving wife, but instead he "spilled his seed" (Masturbated) on the ground. However, God's condemnation of Onan was not for "spilling his seed," it was that Onan refused to fulfill his duty under the law to provide an heir for his deceased brother. The passage is not about masturbation, but rather about fulfilling a cultural family obligation. At one time some Catholics were instructed to use the "withdrawal" method as an acceptable form of birth control. It was impressive in its rate of failure. Once again, it is context, context, and context. Can you say context? I like it when you say context.

As a teenager, I had all sorts of guilt and anxiety around masturbation. This guilt was associated with my Biblical legalistic upbringing and prudishness concerning sex. Often I would be involved in mutual masturbation with other boys from the church and boys out in the country. We would be playing in the hay stack, and the next thing I knew we were involved in sexual things. One of the boys I carried on with experienced a lot of guilt after one of our sessions, and he told his parents about our activities. We got into trouble, of course. What a headache and embarrassment that was! But that didn't stop that type of activity from continuing throughout my youth and young adult years.

We would always justify these actions with the assurance of God's grace and forgiveness! We were told by the older boys that eventually we would marry and that aspect of our lives would be behind us! That would make us feel better when we talked about what just happened. All of us are sinners, we assured ourselves. We experienced the moral guilt, but God was gracious and forgiving.

All of this guilt came from my Biblical legalistic upbringing and people's prudishness about sex. My pastors and other Sunday School teachers viewed masturbation through the lens of Old Testament law and how we needed to live our lives as holy and pure teens. One night on the way home from church service when I was a young teenager, my mother told us kids that she wished she had talked to us more about sexual purity. I believe she thought I was homosexual because of her lack of instruction on sexual issues.

But when I was in my later teens, a youth pastor had told me that masturbation was a normal and natural part of life. This message was confirmed later by my music director when I was in a traveling musical group and ministering in various churches. The music minister told me it is better to masturbate than fall into sexual immortality with a woman. Little did he know that I was thinking about men! He explained how self-stimulation gives release from the tension a single person may experience, especially as he goes through puberty. He showed me in scripture where Paul says in *1Corinthians 7:9* that one should marry rather than burn with lust. I remember him smiling as he added that it's OK to "soap up" while I was in the shower.

To me, as I was going through puberty, masturbating was a normal part of self-discovery. Many Christian guys and boys try to overcome the impulse to masturbate, and they see their inability to stop as a sign that Jesus does not love them.

Today, when I look back on the sexual guilt that I had experienced during childhood and adolescence, I ask myself "Why did I put myself through all that torment?" I wish that I had been given better information.

"As a Father pities his children, so the Lord pities those who fear Him. For He knows our frame; He remembers that we are dust."
(*Psalm 103:13, 14*)

Remember, God is the mastermind behind sex. God created us as sexual beings to enjoy sexual pleasure. Some enjoy sex more than others! Sexual expression is a natural and beautiful part of the bonding that comes from mutual love. Sex was created by God from a heart of love. According to scripture, intimate sexual activity is a gift to be experienced between consenting adults or a husband and wife. And as for those people who don't have such a relationship, masturbation might actually be physically healthy. Medical studies and doctors have said that the semen can be slowly absorbed into the blood stream if it is not released. So masturbation is good! Masturbation is a natural and healthy release for anyone from a medical point of view.

However, for the Christian man or woman, there is the issue of the *thoughts* that can accompany the act of masturbation. Masturbation, while it is a healthy release, usually involves fantasy that brings attractive individuals into your thought life. If physical relationships are not available, the mind engages in this kind of fantasy. In my college Psychology class we talked about fantasy. My professor gave us a series of events that happen in the human heart. He was quoting someone and I had heard this before. This series of events has stayed with me because it can also be connected with masturbation. It went something like…Watch your thoughts, for they become words. Then watch your words, for they become actions. Watch your actions, for they become habits. Watch your habits, for they become character. Watch your character, for it becomes your destiny, just like what Joyce Meyer said. Don't let masturbation stop you from your personal and physical relationships. Masturbation, as a means of filling a relationship void, is the next best solution, even if it is less fulfilling. As Woody Allen says: at least you're having sex with someone you like.

But an excessive fantasy life can cross the border into *idolatry* and *lust* (*i.e.,* uncontrolled or illicit sexual desire or appetite). Just be careful that it does not lead to actions that hinder your spiritual life whether you are straight or gay, Christian or non-Christian. Masturbation to me is not really a huge issue. I think that focusing on masturbation and other issues can distract us from what we're really supposed to be doing.

The crux of Christianity and what we need to focus on in today's world is the Great Commission. Telling others they can have a great life with Jesus! Believers get distracted on specific things like holiness issues and miss the mark of doing what Christians are supposed to do.

Chapter 13
What Makes Me Gay?

Let me tell you that there are some people out there who have had no understanding or even a simplified teaching on the subject of homosexuality. Some of them actually think that an LGBT person chooses to be homosexual one day. That all of a sudden they wake up one morning...and "poof!" they're gay!

These people think being gay is a choice. That people just decide that they are going to live in defiance of the social norms and cultural authority. This makes total sense to me, doesn't it to you? I would not have chosen it, although I am happy now being gay. Who in their right mind would ever choose to go down such a difficult path in our society? The mature enlightened LGBT person simply discovered and *came to terms* with the fact that she or he is gay or lesbian.

So what makes you gay or straight? Sexuality is not the action, it's the attraction.

LGBT people were not recruited to become gay, nor do we recruit others to become gay, as it is so often unfairly stated. We were not even enticed to become gay by being offered some great reward. God, in His great wisdom, created the homosexual person as a homosexual! God created men and women as homosexuals in their mothers' wombs. God knew who we would be even before we were conceived:

"Then the word of the Lord came to me, saying: "Before I formed you in the womb I knew you; before you were born I sanctified you…" (*Jeremiah 1:5*)

It is again stated in *Psalm 139:13* that:

"For You created my innermost being; You knit me together in my mother womb."

God has always known whether you were going to be a homosexual or a heterosexual, because that's how God created you, and approved you! Praise the Lord!

Homosexuals are born gay just like heterosexuals were born heterosexual. Yes, being gay is in the genes. Being a homosexual in this day and age is not only a political and religious question, it's also a scientific one. Remember, statistics say that one out of every ten people born in our world today is a homosexual. That's over 700,000,000 people! Oh, my! One out of every ten people is gay?

So, yes, being gay is totally natural. Homosexuality is found in many parts of the animal kingdom in many species, especially mammals and birds. It is always the minority sexual orientation, but it is there, even when the animals are surrounded by heterosexuality and have the opportunity to be straight. This proves that homosexuality is part of God's plan for natural diversity. But listening to some Right Wing Christians tell it, it is all unnatural and a consequence of sin. So maybe the ex-gay ministries should go to the zoos and tell gay penguins that they are sinners and try to "cure" them, or go to Africa and do the same to gay chimpanzees.

That makes just about as much sense to me as trying to "cure" gay humans.

During my young adult years when I received personal counseling with Christian counselors and pastors, I was always told that the reason why I was gay was because I had an overbearing mother and a distant father. While this may have been true for me, it is certainly not true for every gay person. That thinking was based on a theory of Sigmund Freud which is now regarded as invalid by almost the entire psychiatric establishment. Freud's theory couldn't account for why children in the same family who were treated by the same parents in the same way came out so differently. Some were straight and some were gay, but Freud's theory said they all should have been the same.

I personally think my father just didn't know how to be an involved parent. He would say that I was lazy, fat, dumb, and other negative things. I suspect that he grew up in an environment like that—the sins of the father are often passed down from generation to generation. Yet he did not turn out to be gay…at least not that I know of. This was the case for so many fathers from his generation.

When most gay people think back on when they became aware of having same-gender attractions or "acting gay," it was during early childhood when they had two very involved parents.

While working in various churches I went to several Christian counselors to get their advice on how to deal with my homosexuality. I didn't know how I should handle this personal struggle that I had been dealing with for years. I received all sorts of opinions, including that I should get married. I was told that if I found the right girl, I would be cured of my homosexuality. I actually got engaged on two different occasions when I was in my late twenties and early thirties because of this advice. I was even in the process of adopting the son of one of my fiancées. The closer I got to the wedding date, the clearer it became to me that if I went through with the marriage, I would be ruining many lives, including the lives of the woman and her child. I did not want to do that! I had already emotionally bonded with her son and did not want to hurt him. If a wife and I had children together, they would also have been negatively affected. So I ended the engagements and the adoption process.

Many gay people actually do marry a person of the opposite sex, which is *unnatural* for them, just like it was unnatural for me. This has damaged not only the homosexuals' lives, but also the lives of their partners. Extended families are also affected by this unnatural union.

So, if you are a gay person, think twice before getting married to a member of the opposite sex. Although there are some positive things that might come out of the marriage, the negative aspects outweigh the positive, and the negatives results can be devastating.

In recent years, we have seen several well-known musicians and popular celebrities come out as gay. Often they have been dealing with deception and turmoil for years. While we can celebrate with them about now being able to live authentic lives, their families and their careers have sometimes suffered. You may be blessed to have children, which are a gift from God, but these experiences are still miserable for them in so many ways, and very damaging to all parties concerned. The more enlightened view is to accept who you are and know that homosexuality is in the genes.

In my seventh-grade science class, I was taught evolution and the theory of survival of the fittest. We can assume that since the gay gene has always been with us and has not died out over the centuries, there must be a God-given function for the homosexuals! And remember that most of the homosexual genes are being passed down through the generations *by heterosexuals!* So even if you believe in Darwin's theory, homosexuality has a role in the natural order of things.

Homosexuals do much for the good of humanity. I know that God called me to be a minister/teacher of the Gospel. There are also other people who are called to be teachers, performers, and hairdressers. I also am gifted in all these areas, which helps my community.

I have determined that I am here on earth because I have value. I didn't always believe this because of the attitudes of my church and my family; however, I now embrace this truth. I am here because God created me for a purpose, and perhaps writing this book is part of my purpose!

As LGBT Christians, we believe that we were created with a homosexual orientation, and that it is a gift of God. How would you even begin to replace all of the musicians and singers in our churches who are gay? Who would do your designing and decorating, and where would your actors and actresses be if not for the homosexual community? Who would entertain you if all the gay talent were gone from this world? Even if you are not aware of the strong influence of the gay community in these vocations, they exist and it's something to consider.

We have established that homosexual orientation *is not* mentioned anywhere in the original texts and earliest translations of the Bible. "Homosexuality" is a word for which there is no specific equivalent in the Hebrew or Greek. So I ask myself, "If homosexual orientation existed, and God is so dead set against homosexuality, then why wasn't it mentioned anywhere in the original scripture?" If all scripture is being interpreted and translated correctly, then why is this word only now showing up in today's modern bibles to confuse and misinform people? It's always funny to me when I think about how many homophobic Christians have lived and died by a book that was translated for and dedicated to the public by King James, who was a known homosexual.

In America we still have freedom. We have freedoms to choose. However, freedom is not a license to misbehave or do our own thing. Freedoms are principles to live by. The Bible says that we all have *freedom* to live and love according to God's laws. (*Galatians 5:1*) "It is for *freedom* that Christ has set us free. So stand firm, then, and do not let yourselves be burdened again by a yoke of slavery."

God is not concerned about who you are in bed with, as much as God is concerned about the quality of the relationship you have with that person. God knows and cares about all your relationships. God is asking you, "Is this love?" "Are you caring for one another?" "Are you giving and sharing yourself with that person?" "Are you showing the 'I AM' (God) inside of you to that other person?" God wants to be part of your intimacy on every level.

There are several other important questions to ask. "Are you using that person?" "Are you abusing that person?" "Are you taking from them and not giving back?" "Are you lusting after them as objects and ignoring their humanity?" God forbid, but "are you breaking up another relationship for a sexual fling?" "Is this person that you are sharing your bed with in another relationship?"

God knows what is going on with your attitude and what is going on in your heart and life. God has provided the principles for living and knows that when we follow them, our lives will reflect His nature and we will be successful.

This is my prayer for you and all gay and lesbian Christians who are still living in denial as you read this book: Take a fresh look at what the Bible really has to say about you.

The fundamental problem is not people; it is *ignorance* about sexual orientation, and about the historical and cultural contexts of a dozen Bible verses.

It is my hope to attack the real enemy: ignorance!

My prayer is that your heart will be opened to new truths that will bring you out of condemnation into the glorious light. No blame is on you! Go and err no more! That brings me to my most important subject of all: Grace.

Chapter 14
Grace for Dummies 101

Grace? Wasn't she the wife of George Burns? Say goodnight, Gracie.

As a music and education major at Evangel College, I went through several semesters of music theory. We learned all the principles of how music is constructed. Then after completing all of those courses, my instructor told me to forget all I had learned and just make music! This principle is true for this topic as well. You have learned about homosexuality and the Bible, but now let's set it aside and look at grace.

The "Good News" is that if you have been trying to earn God's approval, you don't need to do that anymore. You already have God's approval!

There are many definitions for "grace." One definition is, "what I need, not what I deserve." I think my favorite one is an acrostic: "God's Righteousness At Christ's Expense" (G.R.A.C.E.).

I define "grace" by what is commonly accepted in most religious circles as "the undeserved favor and mercy of God." Praise God for that, because who knows where any of us would be if it were not for grace!

To those of you who grew up in a fundamentalist church, I am sure you remember the teachings about undeserved favor from Sunday school and Bible classes. Those teachings are accurate as far as they go, but grace is so much more than that.

First of all, grace is a free gift—totally, completely and absolutely. You couldn't earn it if you tried. In fact, if you received grace because of something that you had done, it would not be grace. Grace is the gift that results from God's accounting, or crediting, to you the same judgment, righteousness and favor that He accounts to Jesus Christ.

I am starting to get happy! How about you?

In *1 Peter 2:10* (NIV), we see a great message to today's gay Christians:

> "Once you were *not a people*, but now you *are* the people of God; once you had not received mercy, but now you have received mercy."

There is a song I have sung in church for years that I just love because it includes me! It's called *We're the People of God,* and it contains the core message of the scripture:

> *With our lips let us sing one confession;*
> *With our hearts hold to one truth alone.*
> *He has erased our transgressions.*
> *Claimed us and called us His own,*
> *His very own!*
>
> *We're the people of God, called by His name*
> *Called from the dark, and delivered from shame.*
> *One holy race, saints everyone,*
> *Because of the blood of Christ, Jesus the Son!"*

(Music and words by Wayne Watson)

At this time in the history of the gay and lesbian Christian community, God is allowing us to understand that we are *all* included as a part of God's people. We have received God's mercy. God's grace has been abundantly poured out on us in a spiritual renewal and awakening of our generation.

LGBT people might even be the remnant that God is referring to in scripture when He talks about the Last Days before the coming of Jesus Christ. More than one publicly-acknowledged straight person in the Christian world has prophesied this. On TBN LIVE on 2-28-1989 (www.itbn.org/index/detail/ec), Benny Hinn said that a tidal wave of revival would usher in the last great move of God. This will begin not in large churches, but in the living rooms of His people who were considered a *plague* by the church. God will use homosexuals to speak forth His truth! This has also been affirmed by a prophecy from Kim Clement, a modern day prophet: "Gays would be at the forefront of this last great move of God." (http://kimclementvault.com/prophecyread.asp?num=401&keyword=GAY)

As Paul wrote in *Romans 8:1*:

"Therefore there is now no condemnation to those who are in Christ Jesus."

We should also never forget those memorable words of Jesus Christ in *John 3:17*:

"For God did not send His Son into the world to condemn the world, but that the world through Him might be saved."

This verse is very significant to me. Growing up in a Protestant church, I was taught the verse just before it, namely *John 3:16*, but then we completely missed out on *John 3:17* which is the crux of the entire passage! Can I say context again? This one verse could have transformed my life and so many LGBT Christians in how they acknowledged their homosexual orientation. All of us could have grown up with the knowledge that God was not condemning us. We are instead to be representatives of Jesus here on the earth. Our self-esteem could have been totally revamped had we emphasized the verse in context.

Many LGBT people walk around feeling guilty, ashamed, unloved, defeated, embarrassed, and like damaged goods. They feel condemned by God because of those teachings that claim to speak on behalf of God. This really brings the point home about ministers, pastors, priests of the gospel being judged ten times harsher if they lead their followers astray. We need to be very careful not to misconstrue what God is saying to His people.

"Woe to the shepherds who are destroying the sheep of my pasture." *(Jeremiah 23:1 KJV)*

No church can function without designated leaders. *Acts 14* tells us how pastors and elders are chosen by their qualifications. The main duty of a church leader is to make sure that people are spiritually fed by teaching them the correct Word of God. That is why we need to be so diligent in sharing God's truth accurately, and protecting the people from spiritual error.

If you have asked Jesus Christ to come into your heart, then you are with Jesus today. You belong to Christ and you are going to Heaven! You are not condemned! You can shout right there where you are, if you want to! This is something you can rejoice about because Jesus took care of your failings, wrongdoings, and offenses thousands of years ago. There's nothing more for Him to do, or you to do, that will make it any truer.

Don't let the enemy or any well-meaning Christian try to steal from you what God has already said is rightfully yours!

Don't let anyone try to tell you that you are less than who God created you to be as a homosexual. No one else can define who you are. God says that you already belong to Him, and you have all the rights and privileges of all His children!

> "There is therefore now *no condemnation* to those who
> are in Christ Jesus." *(Romans 8:10)*

Ponder, consider, and contemplate on the fact. There is no condemnation! That will make you happy!

Earlier in this book we talked about the *Levitical* laws. *Leviticus* provided rules for survival in harsh times for the ancient Jewish people.

Today, *Leviticus* is a message of holiness because we are in a different culture. By the way, the Bible is not a book of rules, but food for us to feed on—to know how we can better our lives.

The message of *Romans* is that once people become Christians, they come under a new law of grace and love. The world changed between the time of *Leviticus* and the time of Jesus. No longer was survival of the fittest the commanding doctrine. Instead, in *Romans 13:9* we are commanded to love God first and our neighbor as ourselves.

The grace of God is an ongoing process based on the never-changing truth that *God is no respecter of persons. (Acts 10:34).* By "respecter," the Bible means "discriminator." In other words, God does not discriminate between people. From the moment of Adam's creation in the Garden of Eden until this very day, everything God has done for us has been based on the fact that God does not discriminate.

It holds true then, if God ever did anything for any other human being at any point in time, then God will do the same thing for *you* and *all* other people. God will heal! God will deliver! God will bless! The list goes on and on! There are no conditions on His grace, which is given to everyone freely. You do not have to be straight or gay or black or white or anything else to qualify. It is for everyone! All you have to do is ask and believe on the Lord Jesus Christ and His grace is yours! That's what makes it grace.

The Old Testament Law is no longer the standard we live by today because we live by grace as stated in the New Testament. *Romans 6:14* states "…because you are not under law, but under grace." We see also in *2 Corinthians 3:5-6:*

> "Not that we are competent in ourselves to claim anything for ourselves, but our competence comes from God. He has made us competent as ministers of *a new*

covenant—not of the letter but of the Spirit; for the letter [of the Law] kills, but the Spirit gives life."

Do you understand that message? When you get stuck in the thought processes that condemns you, or if your "Christian" friends want to hurt you with a "clobber verse," remember that they do not support "the *Spirit* of the Law." The Spirit *(not the letter)* gives you life! You can have life and peace as a LGBT person under the "Spirit of the Law."

Today it is accepted by most fundamentalists that the "Christian" is under grace. They say grace is for everyone, yet in their hearts they seem to think "except for the homosexual." That points to the tremendous problem of *hypocrisy* in the "Christian Church" today. The very people who fight for freedom from the Law for themselves try to apply the Law to those they don't accept in regards to sexual orientation. If they were to look closely at what the entire section of scripture says in the context of that one small, incy, wincy, teeny weeny verse *(Leviticus 18:22 "Do not lie with a man as one lies with a woman...")*, I think they would find themselves coming up short. They are obeying what they think is "the Letter of the Law" instead of the true "spirit" of the Law.

James 2:8-10 NIV says:

"If you really keep the royal law found in Scripture, "Love your neighbor as yourself," you are doing right. But if you show favoritism, you sin, and are convicted by the law as lawbreakers. For whoever keeps the whole law and yet stumbles at just one point is guilty of breaking *all* of it."

Ephesians 2:8-9 states:

"For it is by grace you have been saved, through faith—
and this not from yourselves, it is the gift of God—not
by works, so that no one can boast."

We are set apart by grace. Grace is so much better! When
we look at all the laws in *Leviticus,* no one has ever been
able to keep all of them. Everyone falls short of "perfection"
somewhere. Some of today's preachers are inadvertently, or
on purpose, teaching people in their congregations to hate
other people. That hatred is then backed up by some of the
televangelists who preach the same thing.

Not surprisingly, many of my homosexual Christian
friends still have these bad tapes going off in their heads.
They still feel ashamed, condemned, and damned. They
have asked me, "If a person is heterosexual, and does not
choose Jesus, does that mean that they have righteousness
just because they are a heterosexual?"

My answer is absolutely not!

If a person is gay or lesbian, but *has* accepted Jesus as
their Savior, do they have righteousness? *Yes*!

Just because you're a heterosexual doesn't automatically put you in better standing with God than being a homosexual. It is not their righteousness, but the righteousness of Jesus that puts us in right standing. Jesus gave His
righteousness to everyone who chooses to belong to Him.
That's grace! *Colossians 1:12* says, "God made us qualified to
be partakers of the inheritance."

God alone qualifies us to inherit the kingdom of God.
We can't make ourselves righteous. We can't save ourselves.

We need God's *grace* to qualify us to be partakers of the inheritance with all of the Saints. That is through belief in the death, burial, and resurrection of the Lord Jesus Christ.

Furthermore, God has delivered us from the power of evil. We all need God to get us out of the clutches of spiritual death! When God transferred us into the kingdom of His dear Son, it was not because we deserved it, but because of His love for us! That's grace! Whatever we were, now we are changed. We are transformed. None of us stay the same! We grow from glory to glory. Our sexual orientation has nothing to do with it and remains the same. How we live out our lives is transformed by Gods life in us.

Although Jesus Christ has saved us from our sin, He does not want us to continue in our sins. Grace doesn't give us the free reign to do anything we want. Grace demands that our behavior be consistent with love. What is love? This is what Paul says in *1 Corinthians* 13:4-8:

> "Love is patient, love is kind. It does not envy, it does not boast, it is not proud. It does not dishonor others, it is not self-seeking, it is not easily angered, it keeps no record of wrongs. Love does not delight in evil but rejoices with the truth. It always protects, always trusts, always hopes, and always perseveres. Love never fails."

It seems clear from this and other passages in the Bible that a careless or selfish use of one's sexuality is inconsistent with the standard of love.

We still have the duty and obligation to exemplify holiness in our lives. Promiscuity is not consistent with godliness as taught in the Bible. We need boundaries in our lives when it comes to our sexual activity.

If you are an LGBT person, then one boundary in your life is heterosexuality. Your holiness is to be who you are, not to try to be what you are not (a heterosexual).

For the heterosexual reading this, your boundary is homosexuality. You don't want to be something you are not. All of us must understand that expression of our sexuality is much more than whether we are attracted to men or women, it is also how we build our relationships with those to whom we are attracted and love. We are Christians first and sexual beings secondly. All of our qualities have been given to us by God for the glory of God, if they are used properly. Everything that makes us a person is what we should use to develop a godly life. We should strive to develop that godly life.

Through Jesus' death, God gave you power to be faithful to your spouse or your partner. God has provided the capability for you to love your partner with honor and respect. You don't have to be out there sleeping around with everyone that becomes available. You might want to do that, but we need to put some boundaries in our lives when it comes to our sexual activities. God longs for you to be a part of something that is committed, and clean, and whole, and pure. Jesus calls us to be examples of His love. You can be all that as a gay person!

Throughout the Bible, we read that salvation is by *grace*. If you ask for it, God will give it to you. To be terrified that you will be sent to Hell because of your sexual orientation is not the message from God's heart. This is why the ex-gay ministries are so harmful and don't even work. They misrepresent

God's plan. Converting from gay to straight is not possible and makes no difference to your salvation. It is not possible to change your sexual orientation. If even you *could* make the change, you are already acceptable in God's eyes.

There are too many examples of gay people who have tried to convert to heterosexuality with no success. They are often told that they didn't pray hard enough or make healthy choices. There are many former ex-gays who have tried to convert others, and now they are apologizing to the Christian gay community for all the harm that they have caused by trying to do so. I will say it one more time: you are the person God created you to be. He loves you and accepts you unconditionally! Can I get an Amen Hallelu in here?!

So always remember that it is not what God's kids (Christians) say about who you are, but what the heart of God the Father declares you to be. Enjoy being gay! Straights get to enjoy being straight (at least until they have to pay child support), and you get to enjoy being gay! Jesus died for you on the cross many years ago. That was the only way He could proclaim His love for everyone. Anybody who prays to God, asking for salvation through the Blood of Christ, will be accepted, even the LGBT person!

Let me give you some advice that is universal to all people. Put yourself in an environment where you can grow spiritually. Don't hang around the people, including friends and even family, who are continually being negative and critical of you. That sort of environment will keep you from enjoying your life.

I have found that you cannot hang around negative, depressed or critical people and expect to live a positive life. It wears you down. You get tired, you can't encourage them;

they are more than likely bringing you down to their level. Sucking you into their negativity.

Now don't get me wrong. I love my family, but sometimes I have found it best to stay away from them. When you are around people who will not accept you, it only pulls you down. It's a waste of my time. My time is valuable and so is yours! You should find positive influences that will help you overcome the negative bad tapes that keep running in your mind that keep you defeated.

You are of value. Remember that you are also made in the image of the same almighty God who created and spoke the universe into existence. The Bible says in *1st Peter 3:14-16*:

> "But even if you should suffer for what is right, you are blessed. Do not fear what they fear; do not be frightened. But in your hearts set apart Christ as Lord. Always be prepared to give an answer to everyone who asked you to give a reason for the hope that you have. Do this with gentleness and respect, keeping a clear conscious, so that those who speak maliciously against your good behavior in Christ may be ashamed of their slander."

And that's Grace!

Chapter 15
Affirming Who You Really Are!

You have hung in there with me so far. Thanks! Let's take this just a little bit further. It's the preacher-teacher in me! Let me finish this book by giving you a final "truckload of preaching" so to speak.

My desire through the writing of this book is that we can all become educated, informed and spiritually healthy! We need to move beyond the expectations of other people in order to get past this point about being gay and Christian. Here's why:

As a result of the Protestant Reformation, a special doctrine came into play called "the Priesthood of the Believer." That doctrine stated that we who are *believers in Jesus Christ,* which I am, have the ability to open the Word of God, and by the direction of God's Holy Spirit, to allow God to speak to us through His Word as individuals.

While this is a valuable principle, there has been—and continues to be—great harm done by some who claim to speak on behalf of God. Those with an anti-gay prejudice have spoken incorrectly. They have spoken their negative teaching and proclaimed their biases from the pulpit. They have killed people spiritually in the name of God's love.

There is a children's saying that is a lie from the pit of hell! "Sticks and stones may break my bones but words can never hurt me!" Lie! This is a trick of the enemy. Life and death are in the power of the tongue (words) so chose life! (Deuteronomy 30:19)

So what about you? It does not matter if you are gay or straight. Were you ready to receive new information?

We have already discussed in *Romans* where Paul also says:

> "You, therefore, have no excuse, you who pass judgment on someone else, for at whatever point you judge the other, you are condemning yourself, because you who pass judgment do the same things." *(Romans 2:1)*

Paul comes back to the Roman church later and says, "Be careful when you judge other people, because you will be judged in the same manner." The gospels of *Matthew*, *Mark* and *John* say we are not to judge but to love. Do not be fruit inspectors, by trying to spot every little flaw in others!

The "Religious Right" has seldom used these verses of scripture in looking at homosexuals. What they've done is take other scripture out of context and focus in on the few passages that have been mistranslated to condemn the homosexual. But what is known of God is plain to us:

> "For therein is the righteousness of God revealed from faith to faith: as it is written, The just shall live by faith. The wrath of God is being revealed from heaven against all the godlessness and wickedness of men who suppress the truth by their wickedness, since what may be known about God is plain to them, because God has made it plain to them. For since the creation of the

world God's invisible qualities—His eternal power and divine nature—have been clearly seen, being understood from what has been made, so that men are without excuse." (*Romans 1:17-19*)

Everything you need to know about God is revealed, whether you have a Bible or not. You don't necessarily need a preacher or even a Bible to tell you that there is a God. It's helpful and hopefully, both a Bible and a good preacher will help you to understand who God is, and what He wants for your life.

When we judge God's creations unfairly, there is a progression of wickedness that happens that is laid out in *Romans 1:21-23*:

The 7 Steps Down in Moving Away from God

#1. The people who knew God but did not glorify Him.
#2. They did not give thanks to God.
#3. Their thinking became futile; useless, pointless, and worthless.
#4. Their foolish hearts were darkened. They could not see truth any more.
#5. They claimed to be wise.
#6. They became fools.
#7. They exchanged the glory of God for images of idols. These were things they could worship.

As I mentioned previously, I heard a saying from a pastor that I loved and admired that goes something like this: "In the heart of every person there is a God shaped hole that only God can fill."

Feel empty? Ask Jesus to come in to your heart and fill the hole!

If you are an LGBT person reading this information, I want you to ask yourself: Have I put something higher in my life other than God? Do I practice any of those seven things I have just read?

I think your heart becomes more and more hardened if you make a conscious choice *not* to recognize who God is, or to follow His direction. As you move away from making that conscious choice, your separation from godliness takes that downward spiral.

So if you ever think, or if anyone ever tells you, that *Romans one* is talking about you as an LGBT person, then go through those seven steps I just listed and ask, "Am I on one of those steps?" If you are or were on one of the steps, you probably would not be reading this book. You would not be wondering what the Bible is telling you about who you are sexually. You would not even care or give a rip about what Jehovah God even thinks, or what a person like me has to say.

I say, if you have read this information thus far in this book, then you are not on those steps! You are *not* there! You have recognized who God is and you have not gone down those steps.

You may, however, be on another set of steps. These are the steps that I would suggest for your spiritual growth:

You involve yourself in Bible Study.

You involve yourself in Prayer.

You involve yourself in Stewardship.

You participate in the local Church.

You involve yourself in Praise and Worship of the loving, living, Lord God.

You share your Faith.

You are walking in the Spirit. That's Good News!

Don't ever feel condemned for who you are as a gay or lesbian Christian. There is life through the Spirit! Remember what Paul said: "There is therefore now no condemnation to those who are in Christ Jesus." *(Romans 8:1)*. This passage of no condemnation is also in the same book, the Bible, which is supposedly condemning the gay person.

The process of what the Cross accomplished is sometimes hard to understand. We often make it more difficult by adding our own rules and regulations. You are made blameless in God's sight because of Jesus:

> "I am the Living One; I was dead, and behold I am alive forever and ever! And I hold the keys of death and Hades." *(Revelation 1:18)*

The reason this is so important to us today is because in the culture of the Old Testament times, worshippers needed to offer up sacrifices as compensation for their sin. This is a little like the Catholic tradition today. You confess your sin, and the priest tells you how many "Hail Mary's" and "Our Father's" you need to do to be forgiven. Today, as Protestants, we can go directly to Our Father.

Now the blood of animal sacrifices is no longer required. Jesus became the spotless Lamb that completely paid the price. So now *our sacrifice* is that of worship to Jesus Christ, God's own Son. Our praise and worship is what opens Heaven's doors allowing us to enter into the presence of the Lord;

the Holy of Holies. *Revelation 3:21* even tells us that spiritual-ly we sit with Jesus on His throne as He sits beside His Father.

Some of us have had a tendency to stagger or move unsteadily, almost falling, at this promise, or at least I have! Some of us have never waded out into the depths of this concept. We haven't had the courage to walk in the little bit of knowledge that we already know. To me, this is under-standable. No one has ever taken the time to study and then act on the truths of these promises. We still feel the condem-nation that has been taught to us, instead of the abundance of the promises that God has provided for us. No wonder the gay community has not had the ability to receive the knowledge that God loves them and accepts them. That idea is changing, however, in the 21st century as many LGBT churches are being established.

To the gay person reading this: *Let God Bless You!* It should be apparent by now that our ability to operate in the grace of God is linked to our understanding of our righ-teousness before God—righteousness purchased for you by Jesus' sacrificial death. In *2 Corinthians 5:21,* it clearly and loudly says that we became the righteousness of God:

> "God made Jesus who had no sin to be sin for us, so that in him we might become the righteousness of God."

> "We then, as workers together with Him, beseech you also that ye receive not the grace of God in vain." *(2 Corinthians 6:1)*

Do you see the connection? In one verse, the Word declares that we have already become the very righteousness of God. In the very next verse we're warned not to receive "the grace of God in vain." That term in the King James Version "in vain" simply means "uselessly, or to no effect."

Failing to understand that you stand before God completely righteous—robed in the purity and authority of Jesus—will cause you to nullify, invalidate, annul, and cancel out the operation of God's grace in your life. It creates fear, which gives us another acrostic (False Evidence Appearing Real—F.E.A.R). So don't do it!

God in His ultimate wisdom created you! You were created as a gay or straight person no matter what anyone else might tell you. It is a free gift! God wanted you to do something for Him that no one else could do. God still says that He wants to treat you as if you've never sinned. Being gay is not a sin. Being straight is not a sin. God wants to treat you like you are the smartest, holiest, and most beautiful thing that ever existed. Doesn't that make you just want to shout? All this time, God's been trying to treat us this way, and yet we wouldn't or couldn't allow it. We haven't learned how to receive many of God's gifts.

I always tell people that we have a choice. In America, we still can make choices. We have freedoms to choose. This is one of those areas where you can make a choice! So you make the choice. If you choose to be saved by grace, then you need to quit calling yourself an old sinner and start believing in the fullness of God's saving grace.

When you refuse to receive the gifts that God is trying to bestow on you, you reject the grace of God. Make up your mind that you are not going to do that any longer!

I want to remind you again that God is no respecter of persons. Everything that God has ever done through Jesus, God will do for you. Stand up right where you are and Praise Him! What a tremendous promise that is! Everything God has ever given Jesus, God will give to you. Remember:

"If God be for us, who can be against us? He that spared not His own Son, but delivered Him up for us all, how shall He not with Him also freely give us all things?" *(Romans 8:31-32)*

We are joint heirs with Jesus:
"Now if we are children, then we are heirs—heirs of God and co-heirs with Christ, if indeed we share in his sufferings in order that we may also share in his glory." *(Romans 8:17)*

In the church I founded, Celebration of Faith, we quote Bible verses that I learned at another Bible-believing church. We proclaim this aloud at our weekly services on Sunday mornings where the enemy can hear it and our faith can be strengthened by them. We've been declaring these verses at the beginning of our services every Sunday since 1994. I encourage my people to say these things about themselves every day. You should do the same!

This is the day that the Lord has made! I will rejoice and be glad in it. *(Psalms 118:24)*

For great is my God and greatly is He to be praised! *(Psalms 48:1)*

I'm God's Child. I'm an heir with God and a joint heir with Jesus Christ. *(Romans 8:17)*

Therefore, no weapon formed against me shall prosper. *(Isaiah 54:17)*

For the weapons of my warfare, they are not carnal, but mighty, through God, to the pulling down of enemy strongholds. *(2 Corinthians 10:4)*

I am more than a conqueror! *(Romans 8:37)*

I am victorious! Because I walk by faith, and not by sight, *(2 Corinthians 5:7)*

And greater is He that is me, than he that is in the world! *(1 John 4:4)*

Everything that Jesus has is ours, and we access these blessings by faith. If we say, "I believe," grace says, "Have it all."

So let's begin to exercise our faith! Of course, there's no such thing as grace without faith. Grace is there, but it takes faith to activate it in your life. Grace and faith run together, and both must be present in a human life.

The Bible states over and over again that grace and peace are from God the Father and from His Son, Jesus Christ of Nazareth. Grace gave birth to the promise, and peace is its guarantee. It is our access to wholeness and prosperity.

The thing that I am about to say I've heard taught by others. It is a hard thing to teach because we tend to pull away from what God is telling us. God is saying, "I'll treat you

like you went to the Cross and paid for your sins yourself."
On Earth it is written that Jesus did that, but Heaven has it
written down that you did it, too. In the Lamb's Book of Life,
it is credited to you, it is attributed to you, and it is official to
you. You have been made approved.

In *2 Corinthians 8:7,* we are told to "abound in every
faith." Have all of the churches abounded in "every" faith? I
don't think so. We've abounded in the grace of salvation and
in the assurance that we are going to Heaven. We haven't
doubted that. There is room for improvement in abounding
in the grace of faith, knowledge, utterance, diligence and in
the grace of love.

2 Corinthians 8:9 says that Jesus "was very rich, you
know the grace of our Lord Jesus Christ, that though He was
rich, yet for your sakes He became poor, so that you through
His poverty might become rich." Jesus did what He did so
that we would be abundantly supplied.

Sadly, when most Christians and gay Christians hear all
this news, they respond, "I can't wear that. I'm not worthy.
It's too good or too nice for me." But if you say that, do not
be feeling guilty for bringing grief to God's heart in this way.
Instead, receive God's promise of abundance by faith so that
you might abound in God's grace. God *loves* it when you find
out what is yours and claim it for yourself. There is a room up
in Heaven with all sorts of blessings and rewards that God
wants to give you. You, as a child of the living God, just need
to ask. God will provide super abundantly, over and above
all that you ever could ask or even think!

What has been happening in all this confusion about
gays and the Bible is that it can make us feel powerless, help-
less, weak, and ineffective. Many LGBT people are so often

confused about who they are, who they can be, and who they are allowed to be, that they can't move forward in being who God has called them to be: Christians, Ambassadors, and Representatives of Jesus Christ.

Although at this point in my life I will never want to go straight, let me just set the record "straight," so to speak! It does not matter if we are gay or straight. What matters most is that we have a right relationship with Jesus Christ, and with each other. Let me encourage you to *get solid*, get firm, get unyielding in your understanding about who you are as a gay Christian! When you are solid, and your foundation is solid, then no one can knock you off your foundation. When you have that solid understanding, you will be able to move forward with God, and become the person God wants you to become.

When we can get past all this old, incorrect, outdated traditional teaching as gay and lesbian or straight Christians, then we can help our friends, neighbors, and family get past their misinformation as well.

Let me also encourage you to *not* get caught up in trying to change those who haven't come to this understanding. They will just wear you down, and if the truth were known, they really don't want to understand. Plant seeds with them, perhaps. Maybe give them a copy of this book to read, or one of the recommended books listed in the back, but don't exhaust yourself or become depressed if they remain stubborn. My experience has been that the LGBT Christian keeps coming up to this same wall, over and over again. Just leave them alone and let God change their hearts. You have done your part and planted the seed of truth in their hearts. Let the Holy Spirit do the rest. We need to be the men and women that God has called us to become.

Despite a certain deceptive tolerance, homosexuality is still regarded as negative by many people. When the subject of homosexuality is brought up in conversation, over the radio, or on TV, negative viewpoints are often re-enforced. This may cause some LGBT Christians to go back into "doubt mode" about their salvation. Then when exposed to correct new information, the pendulum swings again, and they may get over the doubt again. They look around, wipe their foreheads and say, "Whew! I feel so much better now about being gay. I think I've got it. I think I finally get it." Then someone comes along again on the television or radio, or they read something in the paper, or on the internet, or someone calls them on the phone with that same old negative perception. All of a sudden they take another step backwards. They say, "Maybe I'm not so OK about being gay after all. Maybe they are right? Maybe I have been deceived all this time?" Then the battle begins all over again!

Does this sound familiar? Well, don't feel like the Lone Ranger because there are many gay Christians who have experienced this very conflict. They may get all scared and filled with guilt again about who they are as gay Christians. They question their salvation and whether they are going to Heaven, but then they start back up the hill again, one more time. And this time when they reach the top of the hill, they stay there!

Sometimes, the best thing you can do is to get away from those negative people and put yourself in a healthy, positive environment. God doesn't want us to live in turmoil. God has called us all to peace.

God made your salvation possible. I want you to really hear what I am saying: God loves you no matter what your sexual orientation is. You are very precious and important. You were made in the image of the Almighty God. God knew you and had a plan and purpose for you long before you were even born.

You need to also be reminded that God paid a high price just for you.

"You were bought with a price." (*1 Corinthians 6:20*)

You have value and worth. Live your life to the fullest. You are not here by accident! You have a work to do! You were set apart from the beginning of time. You were chosen by God. You just happen to be gay. The God who spoke the worlds into existence choose you and approved you, and equipped you to go forth and do great things.

I have been told by those who have counseled me, that what I am is God's gift to me. What I become is my gift to God.

I want to close this chapter with a prayer. You can receive Jesus Christ right now! It is no big deal. It is entirely up to you. Just say this prayer. Prayer is talking with God. (You are so lucky and fortunate to be able to speak to God directly!) God knows your heart and is not so concerned with the words you may say as God is with the attitude of your heart. The following is a prayer that you can say out loud or silently in your heart:

Prayer

"Jesus, I invite you to come into my life. Please forgive me of my sins, and teach me how to live for you every day. In Jesus' name. Amen."

If you have just prayed this prayer, then I am so thrilled and excited for you! WELCOME! Jesus Christ has come into your life, just as He promised. Now your journey will begin! Get ready! It's an adventure!

SOURCES &
RECOMMENDED READING

Bailey, D.S., *Homosexuality & the Western Tradition*, 1955.

Bogle, Darlene, *A Christian Lesbian Journey; 2007* and author of *"A Miracle Woman, the Naomi Harvey story, 2011*

Boswell, John, *Christianity, Social Tolerance, and Homosexuality*, 1980.

Furnish, Victor Paul, *The Moral Teachings of Paul: Selected Issues,* 1979.

Daniel Helminiak, *What the Bible Really says about Homosexuality*, 1994, 2000.

Jennings, Jr., Theodore W., *The Man Jesus Loved,* 2003.

Johnston, Maury, *Gays Under Grace,* 1983.

Kader, Samuel, *Openly Gay, Openly Christian,* 1999.

Mollenkott and Scanzonni, *Is the Homosexual my Neighbor?*

Nicholson, Adam, *Gods Secretaries*

Pearson, Rev Joseph Adam, Ph.D. *Christianity and Homosexuality Reconciled*, 2000

Rogers, Jack, *Jesus, The Bible, and Homosexuality*, 2006.

Roscoe, Will *Journey of Men, Masculinities and Spiritualties*, 2007

Scroggs, Robin, *The New Testament and Homosexuality*, 1983.

Sundby, Elaine, Calling the Rainbow Nation Home, 2005

Whosoever Magazine, Candace Shellew – Hodge (Website)

White, Mel, Rev; Dr. *"What the Bible Really says about Homosexuality"*

http://chestofbook.com. (Historians believe that David suffered from advanced syphillis.)

About the Author

My name is David J. Harvey. I was raised in Lewistown, Montana where I attended an Assembly of God church. I attended Northwest Bible College in Kirkland, Washington from 1974 until 1976. I continued my education at Evangel University in Springfield, Missouri where I received my Bachelor of Arts degree in Music and Education. I have served in many churches throughout the United States in a pastoral position. Eventually I moved to San Jose, California in 1986 to begin the quest to discover if the Bible and Homosexuality were compatible.

I am the founding pastor of Celebration Of Faith, Praise and Worship Center in San Jose, California, which was established in September 1994. Celebration of Faith is a non-denominational ministry of reconciliation, proclaiming liberation to all people.

I have worked in various non-profit organizations and completed my Master's program in Business Management in 2003.

I began full time ministry in 1975 as a Youth and Music Minister in the Assemblies of God church in Kenmore, Washington while attending Northwest Bible College. I continued to serve in various Assemblies of God churches in Washington State, Kansas, Montana, and California until founding Celebration of Faith in 1994.

I was honored to be chosen as the Grand Marshall of the 2007 San Jose Pride festival because of my many contributions to the LGBT community and various non-profit organizations.

Celebration of Faith is a member of the Allies of Christian Churches, T.E.N. (The Evangelical Network), Coalition of Welcoming Congregations, and the Santa Clara Council of Churches.

Celebration of Faith currently meets at the Billy DeFrank Community Center, 938 The Alameda, San Jose, California.

Additional information can be found on the web at http://www.CelebrationOfFaith.org

Endorsement:

"This book is a refreshing presentation of the passages of scripture that have long been used as tools against the gay community. David Harvey takes us step by step to a fresh understanding of what the Bible actually says about homo-sexuality considering the culture and context of the verses.

David's personal journey is woven throughout the book as he deals with such topics as being Christian and gay; pornography and masturbation. He addresses the harm done by ex-gay groups and churches that condemn homosexuality as a choice. You will be surprised at his conclusions of God's unconditional love and acceptance for the gay and lesbian community.

Darlene Bogle
Author: A Christian Lesbian Journey
A Miracle Woman-The Naomi Harvey story
Snapshots of History - Through the Lavender Keyhole; Older Lesbians Share their stories

14286788R00113

Made in the USA
Charleston, SC
01 September 2012